CHAPPAQUIDDICK

The Killing of Mary Jo Kopechne

The Complete FBI File

By

Detective and
New York Times Bestselling Author
Mike Rothmiller

No part of this book may be copied without the expressed permission of the author.

ISBN-13:978-1987562026

ISBN-10:198756202X

Forward

This is the complete FBI CHAPPAQUIDDICK file.

These pages are in the same order as found in the file.

It must be noted that the clear majority of Americans believe Edward Kennedy let Mary Jo drown to save himself and his political career. Most believe he got away with killing her.

As a former detective, I believe he got away with it. From Kennedy's delay in notifying police, his selective memory, his unbelievable testimony contained in these pages and the theatrical grand jury which only heard from 4 witnesses totaling 20 minutes of testimony before deciding not to indict.

It's clear that since this occurred in the Kennedy's kingdom of Massachusetts, the fix was in. How much did it cost, we'll never know. All we do know is that Mary Jo did not receive justice.

Edward Kennedy was convicted for leaving the scene of an accident with bodily injury. His penalty, two months in jail—but the sentence was suspended. In simple terms, he didn't spend a single day in jail for killing her. That is not justice.

As you read the court testimony, pay particular attention to Kennedy's highly scripted and dubious statements.

This Book is Dedicated to the Memory of
Mary Jo Kopechne

She Died Because of Edward Kennedy

Mary Jo Died Because of Him

FEDERAL BUREAU OF INVESTIGATION

FREEDOM OF INFORMATION/PRIVACY ACTS SECTION

COVER SHEET

SUBJECT:

CHAPPAQUIDDICK (MARY JO KOPECHNE)

FBI WASH DC

FBI BOSTON
245PM URGENT 7/19/69 AMG

TO DIRECTOR
FROM BOSTON

MARY PALPORKI (PHN). INFO CONCERNING.
MARY JO KOPECHNE DECEASED

ON THIS DATE [redacted] EDGARTOWN, b7C, b7D MARTHA'S VINEYARD, MASS, ADVISED BODY OF FEMALE FOUND IN OVERTURNED CAR IN WATER. TENTATIVELY IDENTIFIED AS ABOVE, WHO WAS FORMER SECRETARY TO FORMER SENATOR ROBERT F. KENNEDY. [redacted] b7C, b7D CONFIDENTIALLY ADVISED THAT DRIVER OF AUTOMOBILE WAS SENATOR EDWARD M. KENNEDY WHO WAS UNINJURED. STATED FACT SENATOR KENNEDY WAS DRIVER IS NOT BEING REVEALED TO ANYONE.

END
CXB
FBI WASH DC

REC-5 94-55752-108
EX-111
JUL 25 1969

66 AUG 1969

CC: MR. GALE
MR. DELOACH FOR THE DIRECTOR

November Third
1 9 6 9

Director: J. Edgar Hoover,
Federal Bureau of Investigation,
Washington, D.C.

Dear Sir: EDWARD M KENNEDY

I talked again this morning to the young, local mortician. He verifi[es] my first letter to you: that in his considerable experience with the drownings in the Florida Canals; he could not recall a single victim [who] did not show some vestige of LIVOR...Abrasions...or some other "identifying marks. (I know of course that you folks noticed this in all the preliminary hearing.) Unless the "exhumation" is ordered: Miss Kopechne's name will be added to another long list of American women who have go[ne] by default in your "Jurisdictional Alibi". I have tried too many time[s] to understand the evanishment of good American traditions: but this bid determination of obliterating records of American women: is particu[larly] irritating since you tell us repeatedly that sympathy in our confused [na]tion goes to the perpatrator and not the victim of our escalating "Social Revolution."

The immaculateness of Mary Jo Kopechnes alledged Drowning (Only a nose and mouth congestion) Has not eluded you Mr. Hoover. The mortici[an] says that it is a thousand to one shot that the girl never went into the windshield and remained quiet in the tonneau of the car.

I have never recognized in twelve, long years, that the FBI has [fumbled a] single trick (Except a Childish "Jurisdictional" attempt...to not give a validated death certificate for ▮▮▮▮▮▮▮▮▮ Unexplainably drowned the Michigan ▮▮▮▮▮▮▮ ▮▮▮▮▮▮▮ Now that you face the larger [enigma] of a U.S. Senator's Midnight enigma...one wonders about your great

Note to Mr. Hoover:

I have to explain again in this national confrontation that your well-worn "JURISDICTIONAL ALIBI", psychoanalytically, is just another unconcious condonation of violence...which you have repeatedly charged to the misdirected sympathies of the American public. .. to the "Perpatrator"

Is it possible, Mr. Hoover that you are getting old like the rest of us...when you let beautiful women drown go with so much impugnity?

(I don't even read the Post-Toastie boxes anymore...and I use to always have a tin-badge and an FBI gun.)

TRUE COPY

TOWN CLERK
STURBRIDGE, MASSACHUSETTS

July 23, 1970

F.B.I.
Washington
D.C

Gentlemen,

The enclosed was received by mail on July 21, 1970.

Dilys A. Reynolds
Town Clerk.

TRUE COPY

TOWN CLERK
STURBRIDGE, MASSACHUSETTS

July 23, 1970

F.B.I
Washington
D.C

Gentlemen,

The enclosed was received by mail on July 21, 1970.

Dilys G. Reynolds
Town Clerk.

ENCLOSURE

CORRESPONDENCE

> Advise Ted Kennedy
> To: RESIGN!
> St. Vincent's Cemetery ← Mary Jo
> 7-18-69

TRUE COPY

Advise Ted Kennedy

To: RESIGN !

St. Vincent's
 Cemetery   Mary Jo
               7-18-69

July 30, 1970

REC-10 94-55752-155

Mr. Dilys A. Reynolds
Town Clerk
Sturbridge, Massachusetts 01566

Dear Mr. Reynolds:

Your letter of July 23rd and enclosure have been received, and your interest in contacting the FBI is appreciated.

Sincerely yours,

J. Edgar Hoover

NOTE: Correspondent is not identifiable in Bufiles. The Crime Records Division recalls an anonymous communication received several months ago of a similar nature which indicated that Mary Jo Kopechne had sent the card from the cemetery where she is buried. The message was similar in suggesting that Senator Kennedy resign.

RWE:ncr (3)

FBI

Date: 5/15/73

Transmit the following in _____
                          (Type in plaintext or code)

Via   AIRTEL
     _____
                          (Priority)

To   : Acting Director, FBI

From : SAC, Boston (66-4051)

RE   : SENATOR EDWARD M. KENNEDY
       INFORMATION CONCERNING

Enclosed are single copies of the following:

Letter to the Honorable JAMES A. BOYLE, from ALBERT S. PATTERSON, dated 9/22/70

Letter to ALBERT S. PATTERSON from SOPHIA B. CAMPOS, dated 10/5/70

Letter to the Honorable JOHN C. STENNIS from ALBERT S. PATTERSON, dated 8/20/71

Letter to ALBERT S. PATTERSON from BENJAMIN R. FERN, dated 8/24/71

Letter to BENJAMIN R. FERN from ALBERT S. PATTERSON, dated 9/3/71

Letter to ALBERT S. PATTERSON from BENJAMIN R. FERN, dated 9/8/71

Letter to JOHN STENNIS from ALBERT S. PATTERSON, dated 7/29/72

Enclosures (9)

VER:MIW
(3)

Approved: _____   Sent _____ M   Per _____
          Special Agent in Charge

BS 66-4051

Transcript of testimony at an inquest
captioned "KENNEDY TESTIMONY," pages
numbered 6 through 9

A 58-page manuscript captioned "ALL
HONORABLE MEN (and WOMEN) -- Or, Perjury
at Edgartown," by ALBERT S. PATTERSON

On 5/14/73, ▓▓▓▓▓▓▓▓▓▓▓▓▓▓▓▓▓▓▓▓▓▓▓▓▓, b7D
▓▓▓▓▓▓▓▓▓▓▓▓▓▓, Rhode Island, residence ▓▓▓▓▓▓▓▓▓▓▓▓▓▓, Massachusetts, was interviewed at the Providence, Rhode Island Resident Agency. ▓▓▓▓▓▓ b7D
is known to the Boston Office inasmuch as he was previously interviewed in the case entitled, "JAMES WALTER MC CORD, aka; ET AL;
BURGLARY OF THE DEMOCRATIC NATIONAL COMMITTEE HEADQUARTERS,
WASHINGTON, D. C., JUNE 17, 1972; IOC (Bufile 139-409; BS 139-164).
▓▓▓▓▓ had been interviewed re the MC CORD case as ▓▓▓▓▓ had b7D
been contacted by E. HOWARD HUNT for the purpose of obtaining
information regarding activities of members of the KENNEDY family.
▓▓▓▓▓ was previously engaged in the motel business, Cape Cod, b7D
Mass. and was acquainted with some members of the KENNEDY family.

Mr. ▓▓▓▓▓▓▓ furnished instant enclosures which he had b7D
found among his papers which he had currently been reviewing. He
speculated possibly ALBERT S. PATTERSON may, in fact, be E. HOWARD
HUNT who, according to information resulting from Watergate, had
allegedly falsified documents in an effort to defame JOHN F. KENNEDY
and ROBERT F. KENNEDY. ▓▓▓▓▓▓ has no reason, other than pure
speculation, to identify PATTERSON as HUNT.

The material which ▓▓▓▓▓ furnished the FBI was b7D
received by ▓▓▓▓▓ from ▓▓▓▓▓▓▓▓▓▓▓▓▓▓▓▓▓▓▓▓▓▓▓ b7D, b7C
▓▓▓▓▓▓▓▓▓▓▓▓▓▓▓▓▓▓▓▓▓▓▓ and ▓▓▓▓ became friends
during the Summer of 1969 when both were working for the ▓▓▓▓▓
▓▓▓▓▓▓▓▓▓▓▓ in Washington, D. C. ▓▓▓▓▓ subsequently transferred to ▓▓▓▓▓▓▓▓▓ Office where he is now an Administrative b7D

* See 139-4059-907

BS 66-4051

Assistant. ▓▓▓ and ▓▓▓ have remained close friends b7D, b7C
and ▓▓▓ note transmitting the enclosures to ▓▓▓ b7D
included the statement it was being sent "for your amusement
and amazement."

      ▓▓▓ stated while he did not know whether the b7D
enclosed material would be of interest to the Bureau, it was
being furnished to the FBI for any action deemed appropriate.

      Foregoing is furnished for information. No further
action at Boston.

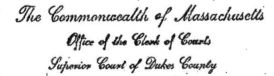

The Commonwealth of Massachusetts
Office of the Clerk of Courts
Superior Court of Dukes County

CLERK OF COURTS
SOPHIA B. CAMPOS (MRS.)

TEL. 627-4668
EDGARTOWN, MASS.

October 5, 1970

Mr. Albert S. Patterson
507 West 111th Street
New York, N.Y. 10025

Dear Mr. Patterson: Re: Kennedy Inquest

    Enclosed please find a copy of the "INQUEST" and if you are satisfied with it kindly send me the sum of $1 or if not, return the copy to me.

                       Very truly yours,

                       Sophia B. Campos
                           Clerk

ALBERT S. PATTERSON
507 West 111th St.
New York, N. Y. 10025

September 22, 1970

Honorable James A. Boyle
Edgartown, Massachusetts

Subject: KENNEDY INQUEST

Dear Judge Boyle:

I have been trying unsuccessfully to locate a copy or transcript of the inquest that was held last winter regarding Senator Kennedy's explanation of the accident and related events that resulted in the drowning of Mary Jo Kopechne, over which I understand you presided.

(1) Can you assist me in obtaining or locating such a copy?

(2) Can you tell me if Senator Kennedy swore under oath as to the accuracy of the explanation he made public via radio/TV a year ago last summer?

Thanking you in advance,

Very truly yours,

Albert S. Patterson

ASP:s

Suggest you write to Mrs. Sophia B. Campos, Clerk of Courts, Edgartown, Mass.

139-4089-2224

507 West 111th Street
New York, N.Y. 10025
August 20, 1971

Honorable John C. Stennis
Senate Office Building
Washington, D.C.

Dear Senator Stennis:

I am in the process of accumulating what I believe to be incontestable evidence, and a lot of it, that a very well known United States senator committed perjury on several counts rather recently, expressed in terms of years.

Moreover, the nature of these perjurious statements and the occasion on which they were made strongly suggest that this senator may have not only instigated but participated in a major crime. If this should be the case, I believe the United States Senate and the American public should know about it.

I also believe this matter should first be brought to the attention of the Select Committee on Standards and Conduct, of which I understand you are the chairman, for scrutiny and further action, if warranted. At the present time, I would estimate completing this work in several more weeks or possibly a couple of months. Rather than sending it to you through the mails, however, I would much prefer handing it to you in the course of a personal interview, perhaps together with one or more others of your committee to be selected by you, in Washington. Naturally, I would like to know, first, if this would be agreeable with you, and, second, if such a trip on my part would not be considered at the "convenience of the government". In short, are funds available to your committee to defray the limited expenses that would be involved for such a trip?

I trust that you understand my position and agree that this is a matter requiring a careful approach.

Sincerely yours,

Albert S. Patterson

ASP:s

United States Senate
SELECT COMMITTEE ON STANDARDS AND CONDUCT
WASHINGTON, D.C. 20510

August 24, 1971

Mr. Albert S. Patterson
507 West 111th Street
New York, New York 10025

Dear Mr. Patterson:

Senator Stennis, as the Chairman of the Select Committee on Standards and Conduct of the U. S. Senate, has asked me to reply to your letter of August 20, 1971.

The Committee would be interested in seeing any evidence which you have relating to alleged misconduct by a Senator. In order for me to determine whether the matter lies within the jurisdiction of this Committee, and to make a preliminary evaluation of the evidence, I would like to have a better idea of what you have before we authorize any expenses for your travel to Washington, D. C. I would suggest that you send me a sworn statement of the allegations together with enough of the underlying evidence on which I can base such a determination. Naturally, this communication with you will be held on a privileged and confidential basis.

With appreciation for your interest in the affairs of the Senate.

Sincerely yours,

Benjamin R. Fern
Chief Counsel

BRF/dbk

507 West 111th St
New York, N.Y. 10025
September 3, 1971

Benjamin R. Fern, Esq.*
 Chief Counsel
Select Committee on Standards and Conduct*
United States Senate
Washington, D.C. 20105

Dear Mr. Fern:

Thank you for your reply of August 24th to my letter of the 20th to Senator Stennis. Since your initial interest has been expressed, I can tell you that the senator referred to is Edward M. Kennedy, of Massachusetts.

I heard the Senator's radio/TV explanation of his "accident" of mid-July 1969, in which Mary Jo Kopechne lost her life from drowning, in the course of which he made one particular statement that, due to certain specific knowledge that I possess, left me with no choice but disbelief. Some time later, I obtained a published copy of the inquest that was held the following winter and I found the same incredible statement made under oath, along with a number of others that I cannot but regard as perjurious, not only on the part of Senator Kennedy but others who were members of the party.

A sworn statement of my allegations together with underlying evidence, such as you request, would constitute what I want to present to the Committee in person and discuss with them, and I hope the reason for such strong preference will become apparent in the light of the following, if it is not already.

I understand your desire for preliminary information well enough, and to provide you with such I am enclosing herewith a photocopy of the last page of the mentioned published inquest that carries the most significant portion of presiding Justice Boyle's official Opinion. If you are not already familiar with the fact, Senator Kennedy stated under oath during the inquest that he had left the cottage that evening at 11:15 with the intention of returning directly to his hotel in Edgartown, after dropping Miss Kopechne off at hers, and that he was unaware that he had made a "wrong turn" until the moment just before his car went off the bridge. I now draw your attention to the fact that Justice Boyle expressed grave doubt as to the veracity of those statements. (What is equally unbelievable to me is that Justice Boyle concerned himself with whether there was "anything criminal in (Senator Kennedy's) operation of the motor vehicle (emphasis added), rather than the Senator's motive for deliberately turning toward the bridge instead of the ferry, as he (the Justice) obviously suspects. Incidentally, after having read only a portion of the inquest, I wrote to Justice Boyle and asked to whom the information should be given if there was reason to believe that perjury had been committed in this inquest. I received no reply.)

Mr. Fern
Page 2 ... Sept. 3, 1971

CONFIDENTIAL

    If your interest is now further aroused, and if you should be interested in reading the entire inquest, it is obtainable ($1.00 per copy) from Magnum-Royal Publishing Co., 1560 Broadway, New York, N.Y. 10036. It has numerous photographs that are helpful, as well as the complete testimony of all witnesses. Should you decide to avail yourself of such a version, I respectfully suggest that you do so in the most "unofficial" manner possible, such as through a private citizen or as one yourself.

    The question has probably arisen in your mind as to why I should have perceived the alleged perjurious statements and why it would seem that I, alone, should have noticed a false statement in the Senator's "explanation." I cannot answer the question. Moreover, it has seemed most unusual to me as well. It is possible that a few others did notice it but considered it more discreet, if not safer for person, to remain silent. I cannot do so. And I will add in this respect that reactions to the inquest from professional observers could be summed up in the way one of them expressed it: "More questions were raised than were answered." It is possible, too, that my having perceived the false statement in the radio/TV account sensitized me to an appreciably greater degree than all the others (?) who read the inquest or were involved and therefore made me more perceptive. To conclude this question from my standpoint, I refer you once again to the parenthetical portion of the last paragraph on the preceding page.

    If you still want a sworn statement from me, kindly prepare the statement based on the information given herein (in duplicate, please), send it to me and I will either sign it before a notary public or use it as a guide to make another in which such alterations as I may believe are in order and proper, and send it to you after notarization.

    Please be mindful that what I wish to present to the Committee is "new light" that I am convinced will expose perjury and offer sound explanation for other incredible statements and contradictions, as well as possibly opening the way, finally, for justice to resume its proper course.

    As indicated in my letter to Senator Stennis, however, I am in the process of preparing and assembling in proper and intelligible order the various statements and allegations referred to that I regard perjurious and unsupportable. There is a limited amount of time I can spare for this work, however, and it is not anticipated being finished before the end of this month. In fact, I have not been able to finish reading quite all of the testimony and I wish to do so in the interest of thoroughness.

    A reply at your earliest convenience would be appreciated.

                          Very truly yours,

                           Albert S. Patterson

ASP:s

PRIVATE AND STRICTLY CONFIDENTIAL TO MR. FERN

United States Senate
SELECT COMMITTEE ON STANDARDS AND CONDUCT
WASHINGTON, D.C. 20510

September 8, 1971

Mr. Albert S. Patterson
507 West 111th Street
New York, New York 10025

Dear Mr. Patterson:

I have your letter of September 3, 1971 but I regret that I cannot express any further interest in your matter until I have the bases of your allegations before me in order to evaluate them.

Sincerely yours,

Benjamin R. Fern
Chief Counsel

BRF/dbk

507 West 111th Street
New York, N.Y. 10025
July 29, 1972

REC'D AUG 7 1972

PRIVATE and CONFIDENTIAL

Honorable John Stennis, Chairman
Select Committee on Standards and Conduct
Senate Office Building
Washington, D.C.

Re: Kennedy-Kopechne Inquest

Dear Senator Stennis:

Included among the several enclosures herewith is a photocopy of a letter I wrote you last August 20th, the present purpose of which is to refresh your memory. Photocopies of sequelae to that letter are also enclosed so that you may have the ready benefit of full knowledge of subsequent developments.

It has taken this long, almost a year, to renew the matter with your Committee for several reasons. One is that, so numerous are the perjuries and so monstrous the hoax of the alleged "accident" and the attempted "rescue", the task begun proved far greater than then envisioned. Not just the Senator in question, but virtually every survivor of the cook-out party committed perjury, if not all. And as I went deeper and assembled and organized the evidence, I found myself facing the duty of writing a full-scale book, exposing the whole affair for what it was. This could not be accomplished in the relatively short time I anticipated in the late summer of 1971.

Another time-consuming task concerned what I then considered a most obvious and flagrant perjury (alluded to in my letter to Mr. Fern). My contention was based on what was regarded some years ago as sound, scientific fact. Nevertheless, I decided that obtaining unimpeachable confirmation from competent and recognized authority would be the best course before making such an accusation openly. I wrote many letters, but received very few replies. I also did further research and discovered that knowledge in the area involved has been extended since it was taught to me. Not that the earlier teachings have been refuted, but modified. I am still extremely skeptical of the Senator's claim, but a retreat of even less than 1% from a previously believed 100% applicability forces me to abandon accusation of perjury on this particular ground. There is no point in pursuing this specific item further--at least, at this moment--and it is not mentioned in my book. Others abound.

Senator Stennis   Page 2   PRIVATE and CONFIDENTIAL

       Also from the standpoint of time, I felt obliged to read two books on the subject that came to my attention late last fall and winter. They are mentioned in my book. Additionally, this has necessarily been a spare-time project.

       So much for accounting for interim time and transpirations. As you will see, the enclosed manuscript is the first section of my book, All Honorable Men (and Women). Although excerpts from the testimonies of a number of others are included, it deals principally with the Senator's testimony. It constitutes about twenty-five percent of the total, which is about three-quarters or a little more finished as of this writing. I believe this is the portion your Committee would be most concerned with, and/or concerned with first. Certainly, it more than satisfies Mr. Fern's request for "underlying evidence" of my allegations of perjury. Where seven outright perjuries are cited and detailed in the manuscript, three additional ones were perceived as my work progressed in sections dealing primarily with the testimonies of others closely associated with him and these additional perjuries are cited therein.

       I reinforce the recommendation made early in the book that Mr. Kennedy's testimony be read straight through in order to gain the best overall view and comprehension of the event as a whole, then go back and look up the perjuries and quasi-perjuries as they are referenced. Detailing of the perjuries begins on page 20, the quasi-perjuries (anomalies) on page 25. "Skim" reading would be a serious mistake.

       You and/or your colleagues may find yourselves wondering about the authenticity of my source. I received my copy of The Inquest from the Clerk of Courts in Edgartown, having been referred to her (Mrs. Campos) by Judge Boyle in his handwritten reply to my inquiry to him about obtaining testimonial transcript. Photocopies of that correspondence are also enclosed.

       At the time I had the title page photocopied, I had anticipated copyrighting each section as it was finished. Then I learned that a restricted and limited circulation of a manuscript prior to publication does not jeopardize copyrightability, that copyrighting a work of this sort implies that it has been made public. I did not proceed with the copyright application and none of the manuscript has (yet) been made public.

       Now there are several other things you should know, Mr. Stennis, the importance of which can hardly be overemphasized. At

Senator Stennis   Page 3   PRIVATE and CONFIDENTIAL

this stage, I can only amplify the contents of the second paragraph of my initial letter to you (Aug. 20, 1971). The information contained in All Honorable Men (and Women), especially the first section, is going to be made public. Whether it will be before or after a Senate investigation/action will depend almost exclusively on the decision made by your Committee. In this connection, it is most important that you know that I have made arrangements for its publication as automatically as possible coinciding with my untimely death or sudden and/or undue incapacitation. Especially under such regrettable circumstances, and to pre-answer the question that is certain to arise in the collective mind of a fair portion of the public--whether you were made aware of it?--my experience with you will be included in the publication. Not only will the publication be made domestically, but in several foreign countries and in more than one foreign language (another time consumer). In any event, the period of secrecy is approaching an end.

As you will note below, copies of this letter, with photocopies of the previous correspondence, are being sent concomitantly to your fellow Committeemen. Additionally, a copy of the manuscript is being sent to your Vice Chairman, Senator Bennett. I regret not being able to provide each, individually, with a copy. However, if strictly private means for photocopying are available to you, you have my permission to make extra copies for those directly concerned with this affair.

Although I provide the answers to a number of hitherto unanswered questions in my book, I daresay they stimulate still others to which answers are yet lacking. I would anticipate being able to answer some of those, but there are questions still incompletely answered in my mind, too. However, I believe the answers are obtainable and my conviction is strong that they should be found.

A few of the questions in your mind(s) probably concern me. For instance, you may wonder at my motive. That can be answered readily in one word: duty. And please accept such assurance as I can give that I do not seek to draw attention to myself. I can also tell you, and you may be interested in knowing it, that in the past I have been given a governmental clearance for Secret. The agency involved was the Navy; the time, circa 1958-1962. I would assume this is verifiable through the records of either or both the Navy and the FBI.

Senator Stennis   Page 4   PRIVATE and CONFIDENTIAL

Concluding for the moment, I now anticipate your agreeing that a personal meeting and discussion of this matter between myself and your Committee would be most desirable and advisable. I can arrange to take the time to visit Washington largely at your convenience, as originally proposed, but would be amenable to any other suggestion you might like to offer. In any case, several days' notice would be preferred.

Sincerely,

Albert S. Patterson

ASP:s

Encl.

cc: Hon. Wallace F. Bennett
    Hon. John S. Cooper
    Hon. Len B. Jordan
    Hon. William B. Spong, Jr.
    Hon. Herman E. Talmadge
    Benjamin R. Fern, Esq.

P.S. Early acknowledgment of receipt of this communication by all recipients would be appreciated.

KENNEDY TESTIMONY

A. Well, Mr. Dinis, I would say that having lived on Cape Cod and having visited these is[...] I am aware some roads are paved.
THE COURT: I am sorry, that is not quite responsive. The question is whether or not you realized the road from the ferry to the cottage was paved.
MR. DINIS: That is correct.
THE WITNESS: Yes.
THE COURT: That is, did you become aware of it during your two trips?
THE WITNESS: Well, I would just say it was not of particular notice to me whether it was paved or unpaved.
THE COURT: Were you driving the car in either one of these times?
THE WITNESS: I was not.
Q (By Mr. Dinis) Well, while you were driving down Dyke Road and after you noticed it was a dirt road and you were driving at twenty miles an hour, what happened, Mr. Kennedy?
A Well, I became —
THE COURT: I'm going to ask one question. At any time after you got on the unpaved road, the so-called Dyke Road, did you have a realization that you were on the wrong road?
THE WITNESS: No.
THE COURT: Do you remember the question?
THE WITNESS: After I realized it was an unpaved road, what did I become aware of?
Q (By Mr. Dinis) Well, after you realized it was an unpaved road and that you were driving at twenty miles an hour, what happened then?
A I went off Dike Bridge or I went off a bridge.
Q You went off a bridge into the water?
A That is correct.
Q Did you apply the brakes of that automobile prior to going off into the water?
A Perhaps a fraction of a second before.
Q What prompted you to do that?
A Well, I was about to go off a bridge and I applied the brakes.
Q Were there any lights in that area?
A Absolutely no lights in that area I noticed other than the lights on my vehicle.
Q Did you realize at that moment that you were not heading for the ferry?
A At the moment I went off the bridge, I certainly did.
Q Do you recall whether or not the — strike that question — well, what happened after that, Senator?
A Well, I remembered the vehicle itself just beginning to go off the Dike Bridge, and the next thing I recall is the movement of Mary Jo next to me, the struggling, perhaps hitting or kicking me and I, at this time, opened my eyes and realized I was upside-down, that water was crashing in on me, that it was pitch black, I knew that and I was able to get half a gulp, I would say, of air before I became completely immersed in the water. I realized that Mary Jo and I had to get out of the car.
I can remember reaching down to try and get the doorknob of the car and lifting the door handle and pressing against the door and it not moving. I can remember reaching what I thought was down, which was really up, to where I thought the window was and feeling along the side to see if the window was open and the window was closed, and I can remember the last sensation of being completely out of air and inhaling what must have been a half a lung full of water and assuming that I was going to drown and the full realization that no one was going to be looking for us that night until the next morning and that I wasn't going to get out of that car alive and then somehow I can remember coming up to the last energy of just pushing, pressing, and coming up to the surface.
Q Senator, how did you realize that you were upside down in the car?
A Because — that was a feeling that I had as soon as I became aware that — the water rushing in and the blackness. I knew that, I felt I was upside down, I really wasn't sure of anything, but I thought I was upside down.
Q Were you aware that the windows on the passenger's side were blown out of the car, were smashed?
A I have read that subsequently. I wasn't aware of it at the time.
Q Were you aware if there was any water rushing in on the passenger's side?
A There was complete blackness. Water seemed to rush in from every point, from the windshield, from underneath me, above me. It almost seemed like you couldn't hold the water back even with your hands. What I was conscious of was the rushing of the water, the blackness, the fact that it was impossible to even hold it back.
Q And you say at that time you had a thought to the effect that you may not be found until morning?
A I was sure that I was going to drown.
Q Did you make any observations of the condition of Miss Kopechne at that time?
A At what time?
Q At that particular moment when you were thrashing around in the car?
A Well, at the moment I was thrashing around I was trying to find a way that we both could get out of the car, and at some time after I tried the door and the window I became convinced I was never going to get out.
Q Was the window closed at that time?
A The window was open.
Q On the driver's side?
A That's correct.
Q And did you go through the window to get out of the car?
A I have no idea in the world how I got out of that car.
Q Do you have any recollection as to how the automobile left the bridge and went over into the water?
A How it left the bridge?
Q Yes. What particular path did it take?
A No.
Q Did it turn over?
A I have no idea.
THE COURT. I would like to inquire, Mr. Dinis, something about the operation of the car, if you are finished.
MR. DINIS. Go right ahead, your Honor.
THE COURT. You are driving along the dike sandy road and you are approaching the Dike Bridge. Now, can you describe to me what you saw, what you did, what happened from the point when first you saw the bridge?
THE WITNESS. I would estimate that time to be fractions of a second from the time that I first saw the bridge and was on the bridge.
THE COURT. Did you have on your high beams, do you remember?
THE WITNESS. I can't remember.
THE COURT. Is it your custom to use high beams when you are driving?
THE WITNESS. I rarely drive, I really couldn't tell you, I may have.
THE COURT. It is recommended.
THE WITNESS. It is recommended, but sometimes if there is a mist you see better with low beams.
THE COURT. Did you see the bridge before you actually reached it?
THE WITNESS. The split second before I was on it.
THE COURT. Did you see that it was at an angle to the road?
THE WITNESS. The bridge was at an angle to the road?
THE COURT. Yes.
THE WITNESS. Just before going on it I saw that.
THE COURT. Did you make any attempt to turn your wheels to follow that angle?
THE WITNESS. I believe I did, your Honor. I would assume that I did try to go on the bridge. It appeared to me at that time that the road went straight.
THE COURT. Were you looking ahead at the time you were driving the car, at that time?
THE WITNESS. Yes, I was.
THE COURT. Your attention was not diverted by anything else?
THE WITNESS. No, it wasn't.
THE COURT. I don't want to foreclose you, Mr. Dinis. I want to go into the question of alcoholic beverages. Perhaps you had that in mind later?
MR. DINIS. Yes, your Honor.
THE COURT. All right.
Q Going back to the cottage earlier in the day, you stated you volunteered the information that you had a rum and Coca-Cola?

-6- 139-4089-2224

A That is right.
Q Did you have more than one?
A Yes, I did.
Q How many did you have?
A I had two.
THE COURT. What time was this?
THE WITNESS. The first was about 8 o'clock.
THE COURT. I would like to go back before that. I think that you said you visited some friends at the Shiretown Inn?
THE WITNESS. That is right.
THE COURT. Did you do some drinking then?
THE WITNESS. I had about a third of beer at that time.
THE COURT. And you had nothing further until this.
THE WITNESS. No, I had nothing further.
Q And when did you have this second rum and coke?
A The second some time later on in the evening. I think before dinner, sometime about 9:15. It would be difficult for me to say.
Q Now, during the afternoon of the 18th did you have occasion to spend some time with your nephew, Joseph Kennedy?
A I might have greeted him in a brief greeting, but otherwise, no. I know he was concerned about where he was going to stay; that he had some reservations and that somehow they had gotten cancelled, but I would say other than a casual passing and a greeting, I would say No.
Q He was at this time on Chappaquiddick Island?
A Not to my knowledge. I never saw him at Chappaquiddick.
Q Did you see him at the Shiretown Inn?
A I might have seen him in inquiring whether he could stay at the Shiretown Inn.
Q Did he stay with you in your room?
A No, he did not.
THE COURT. I would like to ask some questions. You said you had a portion of beer late in the afternoon at the Shiretown Inn?
THE WITNESS. That is correct.
THE COURT. Then you had two rums and coke at this cottage at Chappaquiddick Island some time after you arrived, about 8:30?
THE WITNESS. That is right.
THE COURT. Who poured those drinks?
THE WITNESS. Mr. Crimmins poured the first one. I poured the second one.
THE COURT. What amount of rum did you put in?
THE WITNESS. It would be difficult, your Honor, to estimate.
THE COURT. Well, by ounces.
THE WITNESS. By ounces? I suppose two ounces.
THE COURT. I mean, some people pour heavy drinks. Some pour light drinks.
THE WITNESS. Yes.
THE COURT. When did you take the last one?
THE WITNESS. I would think about 9 o'clock. The only way I could judge that, your Honor, would be that I ate about 10:00 and it was some time before I ate.
THE COURT. You had nothing alcoholic to drink after eating?
THE WITNESS. No, I didn't.
THE COURT. How much liquor was at this cottage?
THE WITNESS. There were several bottles so that I wouldn't be able to tell specifically.
THE COURT. Not a large supply?
THE WITNESS. I wouldn't be able to tell how much. There was an adequate supply.
THE COURT. Was there a sustained amount of drinking by the group?
THE WITNESS. No, there wasn't.
THE COURT. By any particular person?
THE WITNESS. Not that I noticed. There wasn't prior to the time I left.
THE COURT. Mr. Hanify, you have advised your client of his constitutional rights?
MR. HANIFY. Yes, I have, your Honor.
THE COURT. Were you at any time that evening under the influence of alcohol?
THE WITNESS. Absolutely not.
THE COURT. Did you imbibe in any narcotic drugs that evening?

THE WITNESS. Absolutely not.
THE COURT. Did anyone at the party to your knowledge?
THE WITNESS. No, absolutely not.
THE COURT. In your opinion would you be sober at the time that you operated the motor vehicle to the Dike Bridge?
THE WITNESS. Absolutely sober.
Q Senator Kennedy, what did you do immediately following your release from the automobile?
A I was swept away by the tide that was flowing at an extraordinary rate through that narrow cut there and was swept along by the tide and called Mary Jo's name until I was able to make my way to what would be the east side of that cut, waded up to about my waist and started back to the car, at this time was gasping and belching and coughing, went back just in front of the car.
Now, the headlights of that car were still on and I was able to get to what I thought was the front of the car, although it was difficult – and I was able to identify the front of the car from the rear of the car by the lights themselves. Otherwise I don't think I would be able to tell.
Q How far were you swept along by the current?
A Approximately 30–40 feet.
Q Did you pass under the bridge?
A The vehicle went over the bridge on the south side and rested on the south side, and that was the direction the current was flowing, and I was swept I would think to the south or probably east, which would be the eastern shore of that.
Q Some 30 feet?
A I would think 30 to 40 feet.
Q Now, in order to get back to the car was it necessary for you to swim?
A I couldn't swim at that time because of the current. I waded into – swam to where I could wade and then waded along the shore up to where I could go to the front of the car and start diving in an attempt to rescue Mary Jo.
Q Was the front of the car facing a westerly direction?
A I would think it was facing in a northerly direction.
Q Well, in regard to the bridge could you describe the location or the automobile with relation to the bridge?
A Well, your Honor, in the direction of north and south I will do the best I can.
THE COURT. We don't have any map, do we?
MR. TELLER. The bridge runs north and south, fairly close to north and south.
THE COURT. That is, coming towards Edgartown would be north and towards the ocean would be south?
MR. TELLER. Yes, sir.
MR. DINIS. May we use the chalk, your Honor?
THE COURT. Yes, if it is helpful.
Q Would that be helpful, Mr. Kennedy?
A It may be.
Q I believe there is a board behind you.
Assuming the bridge is north and south–
A Yes.
[Witness draws a sketch on blackboard.]
I would bet that that bridge runs more east–west than north–south.
MR. TELLER. Not directly north, but southeast–northwest.
Q Will you indicate, Mr. Kennedy, Edgartown?
A I would rather have counsel draw and respond. I will be delighted to do whatever the Court desires.
THE COURT. It is only for the purposes of illustration.
THE WITNESS. I suppose the road runs something like this.
THE COURT. You are trying to get the relation of the car to the bridge?
MR. DINIS. Yes, your Honor.
Q As you went off the bridge.
A I think it was like this.
THE COURT. All right, Mr. Dinis.
Q Mr. Kennedy, after you emerged from the automobile you say you were swept some 30 feet away from the car. Is that correct?
A In this direction [indicating].
Q And how much time did it take you after you left the automobile to be swept down to about 30 feet, down the river?

A By the time I came up I was, the best estimate would be somewhere over here, which would be probably 8-10 feet, it is difficult for me to estimate specifically, and I think by the time I was able at least to regain my strength, I would say it is about 30 feet after which time I swam in this direction until I was able to wade, and wade back up here to this point here, and went over to the front of the car, where the front of the car was, and crawled over to here, dove here, and the tide would sweep out this way there, and then I dove repeatedly from this side until, I would say, the end, and then I will be swept away the first couple of times, again back over to this side, I would come back again and again to this point here, or try perhaps the third or fourth time to gain entrance to some area here until at the very end when I couldn't hold my breath any longer I was breathing so heavily it was down to just a matter of seconds. I would hold my breath and I could barely get underneath the water. I was just able to hold on to the metal undercarriage here, and the water itself came right out to where I was breathing and I could hold on, I knew that I just could not get under water any more.

Q And you were fully aware at that time of what was transpiring?

A Well, I was fully aware that I was trying to get the girl out of that car and I was fully aware that I was doing everything that I possibly could to get her out of the car and I was fully aware at that time that my head was throbbing and my neck was aching and I was breathless, and at that time, the last time, hopelessly exhausted.

Q You were not confused at that time?

A Well, I knew that there was a girl in that car and I had to get her out, I knew that.

Q And you took steps to get her out?

A I tried the best I thought I possibly could to get her out.

Q But there was no confusion in your mind about the fact that there was a person in the car and that you were doing the best you could to get that person out?

A I was doing the very best I could to get her out.

THE COURT. May I ask you some questions here about the depth of the water?

THE WITNESS. No, it was not possible to stand. The highest level of the car to the surface were the wheels and the undercarriage itself when I held onto the undercarriage and the tide would take me down, it was up to this point. [Indicating.]

Q [By the Court] You were not able to stand up at any point around any portion of that car?

THE WITNESS. Yes.

Q Mr. Kennedy, how many times if you recall did you make an effort to submerge and get into the car?

A I would say seven or eight times. At the last point, the seventh or eighth attempts were barely more than five- or eight-second submersions below the surface. I just couldn't hold my breath any longer, I didn't have the strength even to come down even close to the window or the door.

Q And do you know how much time was used in these efforts?

A It would be difficult for me to estimate, but I would think probably 15-20 minutes.

Q And did you then remove yourself from the water?

A I did.

Q And how did you do that?

A Well, in the last dive I lost contact with the vehicle again and I started to come down this way here and I let myself float and came over to this shore and I came onto this shore here, and I sort of crawled and I staggered up some place in here and was very exhausted and spent on the grass.

Q On the west bank of the river?

A Yes.

Q As indicated by that chart?

A Yes, that's correct.

Q And how long did you spend resting?

A Well, I would estimate probably 15-20 minutes trying to get my — I was coughing up the water and I was exhausted and I suppose the best estimate would be 15 or 20 minutes.

Q Now, did you say earlier you spent 15 or 20 minutes trying to recover Miss Kopechne?

A That is correct.

Q And you went another 15 or 20 minutes recovering on the west side of the river?

A That is correct.

Q Now, following your rest period, Senator, what did you do after that?

A Well, I—

Q You may remain seated.

A All right. After I was able to regain my breath I went back to the road and I started down the road and it was extremely dark and I could make out no forms or shapes or figures, and the only way that I could even see the path of the road was looking down the silhouettes of the trees on the two sides and I could watch the silhouette of the trees on the two sides and I started going down that road walking, trotting, jogging, stumbling, as fast as I possibly could.

Q Did you pass any houses with lights on?

A Not to my knowledge; never saw a cottage with a light on it. —(N)

Q And did you then return to the cottage where your friends had been gathered?

A That is correct.

Q And how long did that take you to make that walk, do you recall?

A I would say approximately fifteen minutes.

Q And when you arrived at the cottage, as you did, is that true?

A That is true.

Q Did you speak to anyone there?

A Yes, I did.

Q And with whom did you speak?

A Mr. Ray LaRosa.

Q And what did you tell him?

A I said, get me Joe Gargan.

Q And was Joe Gargan there?

A He was there.

Q He was at the party?

A Yes.

THE COURT: Excuse me a moment. Did you go inside the cottage?

THE WITNESS: No, I didn't go inside.

Q (By Mr. Dinis) What did you do? Did you sit in the automobile at that time?

A Well, I came up to the cottage, there was a car parked there, a white vehicle, and as I came up to the back of the vehicle, I saw Ray LaRosa at the door and I said, Ray, get me Joe; and he mentioned something like, right away, and as he was going in to get Joe, I got in the back of the car.

Q Is this white car?

A Yes.

Q And now, did Joe come to you?

A Yes, he did.

Q And did you have conversation with him?

A Yes, I did.

Q Would you tell us what the conversation was?

A I said, you had better get Paul, too.

Q Did you tell him what happened?

A At that time I said, better get Paul, too.

Q What happened after that?

A Well, Paul came out, got in the car, I said, there has been a terrible accident, we have got to go, and we took off down the road, the Main Road there.

Q How long had you known Mr. LaRosa prior to this evening?

A Eight years, ten years, eight or ten years.

Q Were you familiar with the fact or – strike that – did you have any knowledge that Mr. LaRosa had some experience in skindiving?

A No, I never did.

Q Now, before you drove down the road, did you make any further explanations to Mr. Gargan or Mr. Markham?

A Before driving? No, sir. I said, there has been a terrible accident, let's go, and we took off —

Q And they went —

A — driving.

Q And they drove hurriedly down?

A That is right.

Q Towards the Dike Bridge area.

A. That is right.
Q And where did you finally stop the white automobile that you were riding in?
A Mr. Gargan drove the vehicle across the bridge to some location here (indicating) and turned it so that its headlights shown over the water and over the submerged vehicle. (Indicating on blackboard.)
Q And what happened after the three of you arrived there?
A Mr. Gargan and Mr. Markham took off all their clothes, dove into the water, and proceeded to dive repeatedly to try and save Mary Jo.
Q Now, do you recall what particular time this is now when the three of you were at the —
A I think it was at 12:20, Mr. Dinis. I believe that I looked at the Valiant's clock and believe that it was 12:20.
Q Now, Mr. LaRosa remained at the cottage?
A Yes, he did.
Q Was Mr. LaRosa aware of the accident?
A No, he hadn't heard — no, I don't believe so.
Q No one else at the cottage was told of the accident?
A No.
Q How many times did you go back to Dike Bridge that night?
A Well, that was the only —
Q After the accident, that was the only occasion?
A The only time, the only occasion.
Q Now, how long did Mr. Markham and Mr. Gargan remain there with you on that particular occasion?
A I would think about forty-five minutes.
Q And they were unsuccessful in entering the car?
A Well, Mr. Gargan got half-way in the car. When he came out he was scraped all the way from his elbow, underneath, his arm was all bruised and bloodied, and this is the one time that he was able to gain entrance I believe into the car itself.
Q And did he talk to you about his experience in trying to get into the car?
A Well, I was unable to, being exhausted, to get into the water, but I could see exactly what was happening and made some suggestions.
Q So that you were participating in the rescue efforts?
A Well, to that extent.
Q You were fully aware of what was transpiring at that time?
A Well, I was fully aware that Joe Gargan and Paul Markham were trying to get in that car and rescue that girl, I certainly would say that.
Q Did you know at that time or did you have any idea how long Mary Jo had been in the water?
A Well, I knew that some time had passed.
Q Well, you testified earlier that you spent some fifteen or twenty minutes of —
A Well, Mr. District Attorney, I didn't add up the time that I was adding to rescue her and time on the beach, the shore, and the time to get back and the time it took back and calculate it.
Q Was it fair to say that she was in the water about an hour?
A Yes, it is.
Q Was there any effort made to call for assistance?
A No, other than the assistance of Mr. Gargan and Mr. Markham.
Q I know, but they failed in their efforts to recover —
A That is right.
Q — Miss Kopechne?
A That is correct.
(Discussion off the record.)
MR. DINIS. I believe, your Honor, before the witness left the courtroom the question was whether or not any assistance had been asked for.
THE COURT. I think the answer had been No.
Q [By Mr. Dinis] And now may I ask you, Mr. Kennedy, was there any reason why no additional assistance was asked for?
A Was there any reason?
Q Yes, was there any particular reason why you did not call either the police or the fire department?
A Well, I intended to report it to the police.
THE COURT. That is not quite responsive to the question.
Q Was there a reason why it did not happen at that time?
THE COURT. Call for assistance.

THE WITNESS. I intended to call for assistance and to report the accident to the police within a few short moments after going back into the car.
Q I see, and did something transpire to prevent this?
A Yes.
Q What was that?
A With the Court's indulgence, to prevent this, if the Court would permit me I would like to be able to relate to the Court the immediate period following the time that Mr. Gargan, Markham and I got back in the car.
THE COURT. I have no objection.
MR. DINIS. I have no objection.
THE WITNESS. Responding to the question of the District Attorney —
MR. DINIS. Yes.
THE WITNESS. —at some time, I believe it was about 45 minutes after Gargan and Markham dove they likewise became exhausted and no further diving efforts appeared to be of any avail and they so indicated to me and I agreed. So they came out of the water and came back into the car and said to me, Mr. Markham and Mr. Gargan at different times as we drove down the road towards the ferry that it was necessary to report this accident. A lot of different thoughts came into my mind at that time about how I was going to really to be able to call Mrs. Kopechne at some time in the middle of the night to tell her that her daughter was drowned, to be able to call my own mother and my own father, relate to them, my wife, and I even — even though I knew that Mary Jo Kopechne was dead and believed firmly that she was in the back of that car I willed that she remained alive.
As we drove down that road I was almost looking out the front window and windows trying to see her walking down that road. I related this to Gargan and Markham and they said they understood this feeling, but it was necessary to report it. And about this time we came to the ferry crossing and I got out of the car and we talked there just a few minutes.
I just wondered how all of this could possibly have happened. I also had sort of a thought and the wish and desire and the hope that suddenly this whole accident would disappear, and they reiterated that this has to be reported and I understood at the time that I left that ferry boat, left the slip where the ferry boat was, that it had to be reported and I had full intention of reporting it, and I mentioned to Gargan and Markham something like, "You take care of the girls, I will take care of the accident," — that is what I said and I dove into the water.
Now, I started to swim out into that tide and the tide suddenly became, felt an extraordinary shove and almost pulling me down again, the water pulling me down and suddenly I realized at that time even as I failed to realize before I dove into the water that I was in a weakened condition, although as I had looked over that distance between the ferry slip and the other side, it seemed to me an inconsequential swim; but the water got colder, the tide began to draw me out and for the second time that evening I knew I was going to drown and the strength continued to leave me. By this time I was probably 50 yards off the shore and I remembered being swept down toward the direction of the Edgartown Light and well out into the darkness, and I continued to attempt to swim. tried to swim at a slower pace to be able to regain whatever kind of strength that was left in me.
And some time after, I think it was about the middle of the channel, a little further than that, the tide was much calmer, gentler, and I began to get my — make some progress, and finally was able to reach the other shore and all the nightmares and all the tragedy and all the loss of Mary Jo's death was right before me again. And when I was able to gain this shore, this Edgartown side, I pulled myself on the beach and then attempted to gain some strength.
After that I walked up one of the streets in the direction of the Shiretown Inn.
By walking up one of the streets I walked into a parking lot that was adjacent to the Inn and I can remember almost having no further strength to continue, and leaning against a tree for a length of time, walking through the parking lot, trying to really gather some kind of idea as to

ALL HONORABLE MEN (and WOMEN)

--Or, Perjury at Edgartown

By

Albert S. Patterson

~~Copyright © 1972, by~~
~~Albert S. Patterson~~

139-4089-2224

WHY'S AND WHEREFORES

"It appears to be appropriate at the outset of this inquest that the reason for its existence, the results that it is intended to accomplish, and the rules of procedure and conduct I am adopting and ordering...should be pronounced...

"'Inquests are, of course, primarily for the purpose of ascertaining whether or not any crime has been committed', says the Massachusetts Law Quarterly, 1921.

"'The primary object of an inquest is to ascertain facts, to decide the question of whether or not criminal proceedings shall be instituted against the person or persons responsible for the death.', Massachusetts Law Quarterly, 1925.

"An inquest is an investigation. It is not a prosecution of anybody. It is not a trial of anyone. It is the duty of the Court to seek out and receive any and all information and testimony which is relevant, pertinent and material to the question as to whether criminal conduct caused or contributed to the death and, conversely, to reject that which is not.

"Although the Judge is not bound by the rules of evidence that apply in criminal cases, it is as much the duty of the Court to decline to receive such improper testimony to the end that persons innocent of any criminal involvement be not injured in reputation.

"For the reasons stated above and because this is not an adversary proceeding, transcript of testimony will not be furnished to the District Attorney or counsel."

Slightly abridged, but with nothing relevant omitted, the above were the words of the Honorable James A. Boyle, presiding, at the opening of the Kennedy-Kopechne inquest, Monday morning, January 5, 1970.

During the next four days, twenty-seven witnesses testified in person and several others--physicians, medical technicians, a physicist, engineers, all with a most impressive professional biography and array of qualifications in their respective fields--testified by affidavit (which, unfortunately, permitted no questioning of their statements). This took more than 750 pages of transcript, and then came Judge Boyle's 4,000-word report, from which the following is excerpted. (The Inquest, p.125.)

"...there are inconsistencies and contradictions in the testimony, which a comparison of individual testimony will show. It is not feasible to indicate each one."

Indeed, there were inconsistencies and contradictions. Some were with respect to certain incidents of common experience given by more than one witness, while others involve self-contradiction and contradiction with fact. The Judge, please note, implied disbelief of certain portions of Senator Kennedy's testimony by stating, a little further on and in view of a list of observable facts gleaned from several of the testimonies (see appendix)--

"I infer...that Kennedy and Kopechne did not intend to return to Edgartown at that time; that Kennedy did not intend to drive to the ferry slip and his turn onto Dike Road was intentional."

...

"I believe it probable that Kennedy knew of the hazard that lay ahead of him on Dike Road but that, for some reason not apparent from the testimony, he failed to exercise due care as he approached the bridge."

I agree with the Judge. There were too many inconsistencies and contradictions to indicate each one, but I think it is quite feasible to indicate and expose a significant number of them, the most egregious and particularly those that can be shown to be either self-contradictory and/or contradictory to fact and which are, therefore, perjurious. Such exposure may enable the reader (including Judge Boyle) to take any of several possible courses: (1) to remove the doubt as to whether Senator Kennedy knew of the hazard that existed; (2) to remove at least some of the obscurity regarding the reason(s) why he did not exercise due care in approaching the bridge; (3) to decide whether, in fact, the Senator drove off the bridge deliberately, or (4) the reader may go back to sleep.

In essence, then, this book is intended to assist Judge Boyle. One of the results of the exposure, however, may be the exposure of some inconsistencies and contradictions (implied, at least) on the part of the Judge (but the Judge is an honorable man--so are they all, all, honorable men (and women)). At the end of the book at least one possible course will be suggested in case the reader asks, "What can be done about it?"

The world knows that this inquest concerned an alleged automobile accident in which, just before midnight, July 18, 1969, Senator Edward M. Kennedy drove off a narrow bridge on Chappaquiddick Island just off the southeastern coast of Massachusetts into a tidal pond and that a passenger, Miss Mary Jo Kopechne, subsequently lost her life by drowning as a direct result.

Much of the world knows that the inquest was held in secret. It was so secret, in fact, that, as indicated in the Judge's opening remarks, transcripts of testimony were denied the District Attorney. Not so much of the world knows that the inquest was postponed four months, and only a little of the world knows, I suspect, that the inquest has now been made public and is available to all. Copies may be obtained ($1.00) by writing to the publisher: Magnum-Royal Publications, Inc., 1560 Broadway, New York, N.Y. 10036. This is the principal source--The Inquest--of the information about to be given. It is in magazine form, and references to specific statements in various testimonies will be made to page numbers therein, as on the preceding page.

Two other books, to my knowledge, have previously appeared on this broad subject. The first was The Bridge at Chappaquiddick (Little, Brown & Co., Boston, in hardcover), by Jack Olsen, a senior editor of Time, who did a remarkable job of researching and then recounting it most entertainingly. No reference was made to the inquest and it is most probable that he wrote it prior to the inquest, or in the fall of 1969.

The second was Teddy Bare (Western Islands, Belmont, Mass.), by Zad Rust, which was written not only after the inquest, but after the emasculated Grand Jury session held another four months after the inquest. Where Olsen devoted his literary talents to the pre-accident Kennedy clan, including Teddy's Harvard ouster and typical Kennedy incidents and anecdotes, the circumstances leading up to the accident and its aftermath, plus his own absolutely unique hypothesis of how the "accident" might have happened (and I wonder if he will continue to believe so, if he still does, after he reads this book, if he does), Rust concentrated on the inquest and the behind-the-scenes goings-on that may very well have occurred. It is a devastating indictment of the Massachusetts judiciary, naming individual judges above Judge Boyle, but, in my opinion, it does not strip Teddy "bare". Both books are highly recommended to Kennedy-watchers and to any and all having an interest in this tragedy or in the cause of justice. The former will probably be found in many libraries, if not bookshops, while the latter is available at most American Opinion bookstores (look in your telephone directory) in paperback at $2.00. Otherwise, the publisher can provide. Such is the scanty bibliography herein. Both books will be referred to from time to time.

In the preceding excerpted quotations from The Inquest, as well as in all the following, all indications of emphasis have been added. Abridgement has been for the sake of coherence. Tedious and unnecessary repetition has been eliminated for ease in reading, as well as irrelevancies regarding the selected exposures and basic facts. For example, there are numerous instances where answers given were repeated in the form of another question, only to be reaffirmed. Those questioning accuracy of either content or intent may avail themselves of an essentially unexpurgated copy from the source given.

Since Senator Kennedy is the surviving principal in this drama, on whom all other testimonies are merely ancillary, and since he also testified first, his testimony will be given first here. And, let it be remembered, Senator Kennedy is an honorable man—so are they all, all, honorable men (and women).

Footnotes will be indicated in the customary manner. Perjuries will be indicated by Roman numerals in brackets and will be discussed fully, or sufficiently, in a section immediately following testimony, while other statements of an unusual nature, such as might fall short of actual perjury, yet lack credibility, or warrant special comment, will be indicated by Roman letters in brackets and discussed similarly.

District Attorney Edmund Dinis put the questions to Mr. Kennedy, indicated by "Q", while the Senator's answers are indicated by "A". From time to time throughout the inquest, Judge Boyle interposed with questions of his own, his questions being slightly indented and preceded by the words, THE COURT.

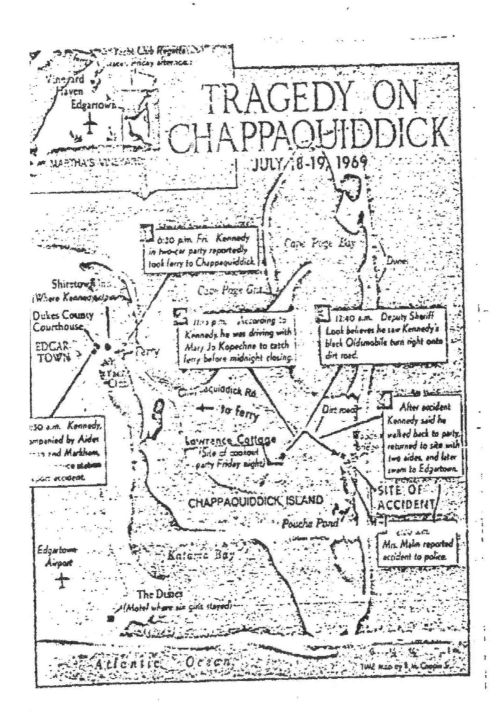

COMMONWEALTH OF MASSACHUSETTS

Dukes, ss.

Edgartown District Court

Edgartown, Massachusetts
Monday, January 5, 1970

FIRST DAY

THE TESTIMONY
OF
EDWARD M. KENNEDY

THE COURT: Senator, would you take the witness stand?
SENATOR KENNEDY: Yes.

EDWARD M. KENNEDY, Sworn

EXAMINATION BY MR. DINIS:

Q: Please give your name to the Court.
A: Edward Moore Kennedy.
Q: And where is your legal residence, Mr. Kennedy?
A: 3 Charles River Square, Boston.
Q: Directing your attention to July 18, 1969, were there plans made by you to have a gathering on Martha's Vineyard Island?
A: There were plans to participate in an annual sailing regatta in Edgartown on Friday, July 18th and Saturday, July 19th, and with my cousin Joe Gargan, Mr. Markham, Mr. LaRosa and a number of other people.[1]
Q: Could you tell the Court what your activities were during that afternoon from the time of your arrival?
A: Well, I arrived shortly after 1 o'clock on July 18th, was met by Mr. John B. Crimmins, driven through town, traveled by ferry to Chappaquiddick Island to a small cottage there where I changed into a bathing suit, later visited the beach on I imagine the east side of that island for a brief swim, returned to the cottage and changed into another bathing suit, returned to the ferry slip and waded out to my boat, later participated in a race which ended approximately 6 o'clock.
Q: When did you check into the Shiretown Inn that day?
A: Sometime after 6:30, before 7 o'clock.
Q: What were your activities after that?
A: I returned to my room, washed up briefly and returned to Chappaquiddick Island.
Q: Now, were you familiar with the island of Chappaquiddick?
A: Never been on Chappaquiddick Island before that day.
THE COURT: You said you took a swim on Chappaquiddick Island Friday afternoon?

---

[1] A neat evasion, the first crack out of the box. The question was whether Mr. Kennedy had made such plans, obviously with the cook-out in mind. The Senator, however, spoke merely of "plans" involving a number of people "to participate in a sailing regatta."

THE WITNESS: Yes, I did.
THE COURT: What automobile was being used at that time?
THE WITNESS: A four-door Oldsmobile 88.
THE COURT: Who drove you to the beach?
THE WITNESS: Mr. Crimmins.
THE COURT: Was the car operated over the Dike Bridge or was it left on the side?
THE WITNESS: No, it was operated over the Dike Bridge.

Q: Was there anyone at the cottage when you arrived there at 7:30 p.m.?
A: No, I don't believe so.
Q: Were there any other automobiles at that house that afternoon?
A: One other vehicle, so there were two in total to the best of my knowledge.
Q: Did you plan to stay overnight?
A: No, I did not.
Q: What transpired after you arrived at the cottage?
A: I took a bath in the tub, which was not available at the Shiretown Inn, and soaked my back; I later was joined by Mr. Markham, who arrived some time about 8 o'clock, engaged in conversation with Mr. Markham until about 8:30, and the rest of the group arrived at 8:30 or shortly thereafter.
Q: Now, did you have dinner at the cottage?
A: Well, at 8:30 the rest of the group arrived and were made to feel relaxed and at home, were served a drink, those who wanted them, and steaks were cooked on an outdoor burner by Mr. Gargan at about quarter of 10, I would think.
Q: Did you have occasion to leave the cottage at any time during that evening?
A: That is correct. Two different occasions.
Q: Would you please tell us about the first time?
A: The first I left at approximately 11:15 and I left a second time, sometime after midnight, by my best judgment it would be approximately 12:15. I left the immediate vicinity of the cottage which was probably fifteen or twenty feet outside the front door.
Q: Now, when you left on the first occasion, were you alone?
A: I was not alone.
Q: And who was with you?
A: Miss Mary Jo Kopechne.
Q: Anyone else?
A: No. [A]
Q: Do you know how she arrived?
A: To my best knowledge she arrived in a white Valiant that brought some of the people to that party.
Q: Do you know who owned that car?
A: I believe it was a rented car.
Q: When you left with Miss Kopechne, had you had any prior conversation with her?
A: Yes, I had. At 11:15 I was talking with Miss Kopechne. I noticed the time, desired to leave and return to the Shiretown Inn and indicated to her that I was leaving and returning to town. She indicated to me that she was desirous of leaving, if I would be

kind enough to drop ⬤r back at her hotel. I ⬤d, well, I'm leaving immediately; spoke with Mr. Crimmins, requested the keys to the car and left at that time.

Q: Does Mr. Crimmins usually drive your car or drive you?
A: On practically every occasion.

Q: Was there anything in particular that changed those circumstances at this particular time?
A: Only that Mr. Crimmins, as well as some of the other fellows, were concluding their meal, enjoying the fellowship, and it didn't appear necessary to require him to bring me back to Edgartown.

Q: And when you left the house at Chappaquiddick at 11:15, you were driving?
A: That is correct.

Q: And where was Miss Kopechne seated?
A: In the front seat. [B]

Q: Was there any other person in the car at that time?
A: No.

Q: Was there any other item, thing, or object in the car at that time of any size?
A: Well, not to my knowledge at that particular time. [C]

Q: And on leaving the cottage, where did you go?
A: Well, I traveled down, I believe it is Main Street, took right on Dike Road and drove off the bridge at Dike Bridge.

Q: Did you at any time drive into Cemetery Road?
A: At no time did I drive into Cemetery Road.

Q: Did you pass any other vehicle at that time?
A: I passed no other vehicle at that time and I saw no other person and I did not stop the car at any time between the time I left the cottage and went off the bridge.

Q: Do you recall how fast you were driving when you made the right on Dike Bridge?
A: No. I would say approximately seven or eight miles an hour.

Q: And what were the lighting conditions and weather conditions?
A: There was a reasonable amount of humidity. The night was clear, extremely dark.

Q: Were the windows opened or closed of the automobile?
A: Some of the windows were open and some were closed.

THE COURT: What about the window on your side?
THE WITNESS: I would expect it was open.
THE COURT: You don't remember that?
THE WITNESS: I don't remember that.
THE COURT: Was it a warm night?
THE WITNESS: I would think it was cool at that hour.

Q: Well, Mr. Kennedy, was the window on the driver's side open?
A: Yes, it was. [I]

Q: And you have no recollection as to the windows on the passenger's side?
A: No, I really don't.

Q: How fast were you driving on Dike Road?
A: Approximately twenty miles an hour. [II]

Q: Well, were you aware at the time that you were driving on a dirt road when you turned onto Dike Road?
A: I don't remember any specific time when I knew I was driving on an unpaved road. I was generally aware sometime that it was unpaved.

aware that--the water rushing in and the blackness. I knew that
I was; I felt I was upside-down. [F] I really wasn't sure of
anything, but I thought I was upside down.

Q: Were you aware that the windows on the passenger's side
were smashed?
A: I wasn't aware of it at the time.
Q: Were you aware that there was any water rushing in on the
passenger's side?
A: There was complete blackness. Water seemed to rush in from
every point--from the windshield, from underneath me, above me.
It almost seemed like you couldn't hold the water back with your
hands. 5/ What I was conscious of was the rushing of the water,
the blackness, the fact that it was impossible to even hold it
back.
Q: Did you make any observations of the condition of Miss Ko-
pechne at that time?
A: At what time? 6/
Q: When you were thrashing around in the car.
A: Well, at the moment I was thrashing around I was trying to
find a way that we both could get out of the car, and at some time
after I tried the door and the window I became convinced I was
never going to get out.
Q: Was the window closed at that time?
A: The window was open.
Q: On the driver's side?
A: That's correct.
Q: And did you go through the window to get out of the car?
A: I have no idea in the world how I got out of that car. 7/
Q: Do you have any recollection as to how the automobile left
the bridge and went over into the water?
A: No.
Q: Did it turn over?
A: I have no idea. [V]

THE COURT: I would like to inquire something about the
operation of the car. Now, can you describe to me what you
saw, what you did, what happened from the point when you first
saw the bridge?
THE WITNESS: I would estimate that time to be fractions
of a second from the time that I first saw the bridge and was
on the bridge.
THE COURT: Did you have on your high beams?
THE WITNESS: I can't remember.
THE COURT: It is recommended.
THE WITNESS: It is recommended, but sometimes if there is
a mist you see better with low beams. 8/
THE COURT: Did you see that it was at an angle to the
road?
THE WITNESS: The bridge was at an angle to the road?

5/ The reader is requested to contemplate this statement, including the
qualifying word, "almost".
6/ The question was most complex and abstruse, of course.
7/ I have. See page 56.
8/ Just what was the purpose of this verbal game? Minutes before, he had
said the night was clear (emphasized, page 6).

THE COURT: Yes.
THE WITNESS: Just before going on it I saw that. 9/ [G]
THE COURT: Did you make any attempt to turn your wheels to follow that angle?
THE WITNESS: I believe I did, your Honor. I would <u>assume</u> that I did try to go on the bridge. [H] It appeared to <u>me at the</u> time that the road went straight.
THE COURT: Were you looking ahead at the time you were driving the car?
THE WITNESS: Yes, I was.
THE COURT: Your attention wasn't diverted by anything else?
THE WITNESS: No, it wasn't. 10/

Q: Going back to the cottage earlier in the day, you stated-- you volunteered the information that you had a rum and Coca-Cola?
A: That is right.
Q: How many did you have?
A: Two. The first was about 8 o'clock. The second some time later on in the evening. I think before dinner, about 9:15.
THE COURT: What amount of rum did you put in?
THE WITNESS: I suppose two ounces.
THE COURT: You had nothing alcoholic to drink after eating?
THE WITNESS: No, I didn't.
THE COURT: Were you at any time that evening under the influence of alcohol?
THE WITNESS: Absolutely not.
THE COURT: In <u>your opinion</u>, would you be sober at the time that you operated the motor vehicle to the Dike Bridge?
THE WITNESS: Absolutely sober. [J]

Q: Senator Kennedy, what did you do immediately following your release from the automobile?
A: I was swept away by the tide that was flowing at an extraordinary rate through that narrow cut there [VI] and was swept along by the tide and called Mary Jo's name until I was able to make my way to what would be the <u>east</u> side of that cut, waded up to about my waist and started back to the car, at this time gasping and belching and coughing, went back just in front of the car.
Now, the <u>headlights of that car were still on</u> and I was able to get to what I thought was the front of the car, although it was difficult, and I was <u>able to identify the front</u> of the car by the <u>lights themselves</u>. Otherwise, I don't think I would be able to tell.
Q: How far were you swept along by the current?
A: Approximately 30 or 40 feet.
Q: Now, in order to get back to the car, was it necessary for you to swim?
A: I couldn't swim at that time because of the current. I waded into--swam to where I could wade and then waded along the

---

9/ Then why did he ask the preceding question?

10/ The reader is urged to obtain a copy of the Aug. 1, 1969, issue of Time and look at the photo of the bridge (p. 13) taken from an estimated distance of some 60 feet on a very dark night through the windshield of a similar automobile.

shore to where I could go to the front of the car and start diving in an attempt to rescue Mary Jo. [K]

Q: Was the front of the car facing a westerly direction?
A: I would think it was facing a northerly direction.
Q: Well, in regard to the bridge, could you describe the location of the automobile with relation to the bridge?
  THE COURT: We don't have a map, do we?
  THE CLERK: The bridge runs fairly close to north and south.
Q: I believe there is a board behind you. Assuming the bridge is north and south--
A: Yes. (Draws sketch on a blackboard.)
   I would bet that that bridge runs more east-west than north-south. [L]
Q: Will you indicate Edgartown, Mr. Kennedy?
A: I suppose the road runs something like this.
Q: As you went off the bridge--
A: I think it was like this. (The relationship of the car to the bridge.)
Q: After you emerged from the automobile, you say you were swept some 30 feet away from the car...
A: In this direction. (Indicating.)
Q: And how much time did it take you after you left the automobile to be swept down to about 30 feet?
A: By the time I came up, I was--the best estimate would be somewhere over here, which would be probably eight or ten feet. It is difficult for me to estimate specifically, and I think by the time I was able at least to regain my strength, I would say it is about thirty feet, after which time I swam in this direction until I was able to wade, and wade back up here to this point here, and went over to the front of the car, where the front of the car was, and crawled over to here, dove here, and the tide would sweep out this way there, and then I dove repeatedly from this side until, I would say, the end, and then I will be swept away the first couple of times, again back over to this side, I would come back again and again to this point here, or try perhaps the third or fourth time to gain entrance to some area here until, at the very end when I couldn't hold my breath any longer, I was breathing so heavily it was down to just a matter of seconds. I would hold my breath and I could barely get underneath the water. I was just able to hold onto the metal undercarriage here, and the water itself came right out to where I was breathing and I could hold on, I knew that I just could not get under water any more. 11/

Q: And you were fully aware at that time of what was transpiring?

11/ Read Mr. Dinis's question again, then Mr. Kennedy's reply the second time and see if you think the question was answered.

Additional notes: (a) This particular account has not been abridged. Any deviation from the Senator's actual words is the fault either of the court stenographer, the publisher of The Inquest or the present publisher.

(b) Just what he meant by "the water itself came right out to where I was breathing and I could hold on" falls short of being altogether clear. But then, they have peculiar water around Martha's Vineyard; you can't hold it back even with your hands.

A: Well, I was fully aware that I was trying to get the girl out of that car and I was fully aware that I was doing everything I possibly could to get her out of the car and I was fully aware at that time that my head was throbbing and my neck was aching and I was breathless, and at that time, the last time, hopelessly exhausted.

THE COURT: May I ask you some questions here about the depth of the water?

THE WITNESS: No, it was not possible to stand. The highest level of the car to the surface were the wheels and the undercarriage itself when I held onto the undercarriage and the tide would take me down. It was up to here (indicating). [M] *this point*

THE COURT: You were not able to stand up at any point around any portion of that car?

THE WITNESS: Yes.

Q: Mr. Kennedy, how many times did you make an effort to submerge and get into the car?

A: I would say seven or eight times. At the last point, I didn't have the strength even to come down even close to the window or the door.

Q: And how much time was used in these efforts?

A: I would think probably 15 or 20 minutes.

Q: And did you then remove yourself from the water?

A: Well, in the last dive I lost contact with the vehicle again and I started to come down this way here and I let myself float and came over to this shore and I came onto this shore here, and I sort of crawled and staggered up some place in here and was very exhausted and spent on the grass.[12]

Q: On the west bank of the river?

A: Yes.

Q: And how long did you spend resting?

A: I suppose the best estimate would be 15 or 20 minutes.

Q: Now, did you say earlier you spent 15 or 20 minutes trying to recover Miss Kopechne?

A: That is correct.

Q: And you spent another 15 or 20 minutes recovering?

A: Now, following your rest period, what did you do?

Q: I went back to the road and I started down the road and it was extremely dark and I could make out no form or shapes or figures, and the only way that I could even see the path of the road was looking down the silhouettes of the trees on the two sides, and I could watch the silhouette of the trees on the two sides and I started going down that road, walking, trotting, jogging, stumbling, as fast as I possibly could.

Q: Did you pass any houses with lights on?

A: Not to my knowledge; never saw a cottage with a light on it. [N]

Q: And did you then return to the cottage where your friends had gathered?

A: That is correct.

Q: And how long did it take you to make that walk?

---

[12] See Perjury No. 6.

A: I would say (approximately 15 minutes.
Q: And when you arrived at the cottage, did you speak to anyone there?
A: Well, I came up to the cottage. There was a car parked there, a white vehicle, and as I came up to the back of the vehicle I saw Ray LaRosa at the door and I said, "Ray, get me Joe (Gargan)." And he mentioned something like, "Right away", and as he was going in to get Joe I got in the back of the car.
Q: Did Joe come to you, and did you have conversation with him?
A: Yes. I said, "You had better get Paul (Markham), too."
Q: What happened after that?
A: Well, Paul came out, got in the car. I said, "There has been a terrible accident; we have to go." And we took off down the Main Road there.
Q: How long had you known Mr. LaRosa prior to this evening?
A: Eight or ten years.
Q: Did you have any knowledge that Mr. LaRosa had some experience in skin-diving?
A: No, I never did.
Q: Now, before you drove down the road, did you make any further explanations to Mr. Gargan or Mr. Markham?
A: Before driving? No, sir. I said, "There has been a terrible accident. Let's go!" And we took off--
Q: Towards the Dike Bridge area?
A: That is right. 13/
Q: And where did you finally stop the white automobile you were riding in?
A: Mr. Gargan drove the vehicle across the bridge to some location here (indicating) and turned it so that its headlights shown over the water and over the submerged vehicle.
Q: And what happened?
A: Mr. Gargan and Mr. Markham took off all their clothes, dove into the water repeatedly to try and save Mary Jo.
Q: Now, do you recall what particular time (it was)?
A: I believe that I looked at the Valiant's clock and believe it was 12:20.
Q: Now, Mr. LaRosa remained at the cottage?
A: Yes, he did.
Q: Was Mr. LaRosa aware of the accident?
A: No, he hadn't heard--no, I don't believe so.
Q: No one else at the cottage was told of the accident?
A: No.
Q: Now, how long did Mr. Markham and Mr. Gargan remain there with you?
A: I would think about 45 minutes.
Q: And were they unsuccessful in entering the car?
A: Well, Mr. Gargan got half-way in the car. When he came out he was scraped all the way from his elbow; underneath his arm was all bruised and bloodied [0] and this is the one time that he was

---

13/ How did Mr. Gargan know just where to go? Note that Mr. Kennedy had just been asked if he had made any further explanations and he said "No."

able to gain entrance into the car itself.14/

Q: And did he talk to you about his experience in trying to get into the car?

A: Well, I was unable to, being exhausted, to get into the water, but I could see exactly what was happening and made some suggestions.15/

Q: So that you were participating in the rescue efforts?

A: Well, to that extent.

Q: Did you have any idea how long Mary Jo had been in the water?

A: Well, I knew that some time had passed.

Q: Was it fair to say that she had been in the water about an hour?

A: Yes, it is.

Q: Was there any effort made to call for assistance?

A: No, other than the assistance of Mr. Gargan and Mr. Markham.

Q: Was there any reason why no additional assistance was asked for?

A: Was there any reason? 16/

Q: Yes, was there any particular reason why you did not call either the police or the fire department?

A: Well, I intended to report it to the police.

THE COURT: That is not quite responsive to the question.

THE WITNESS: I intended to call for assistance and to report the accident to the police within a few short moments after going back into the car.

Q: And did something prevent this?

A: Yes.

Q: What was that?

A: With the Court's indulgence, to prevent this, if the Court would permit me I would like to be able to relate to the Court the immediate period following the time that Mr. Gargan, Markham and I got back in the car.

THE COURT: I have no objection.

THE WITNESS: Responding to the question of the District Attorney--at some time, I believe it was about 45 minutes after Gargan and Markham dove, they likewise became exhausted and no further diving efforts appeared to be of any avail and they so indicated to me and I agreed. So they came out of the water and came back into the car and said to me, Mr. Markham and Mr. Gargan at different times as we drove down the road towards the ferry that it was necessary to report this accident.17/ A lot of different thoughts came into my mind at that time about how I was going to really to be able to call Mrs. Kopechne at some time in the middle of the night to tell her that her daughter was drowned, to be able to call my own mother and my own father, relate to them, my wife, and I even--even though I knew that Mary Jo Kopechne was dead and believed firmly that she was in the back of that car [P] I willed that she remain alive.

14/ But was somehow unable to establish contact with Mary Jo?

15/ Remember the "pitch blackness" he claimed a few minutes ago while under water himself, despite the headlights being on?

16/ Another of those complex and abstruse questions from Mr. Dinis.

17/ Rather than calling for professional help?

As we drove down that road I was almost looking out the front window and windows trying to see her walking down that road. I related this to Gargan and Markham and they said they understood this feeling, but it was necessary to report it. And about this time we came to the ferry crossing and I got out of the car and we talked there just a few minutes. I just wondered how all this could possibly have happened. I also had sort of a thought and the wish and desire and the hope that suddenly this whole accident would disappear, and they reiterated that this has to be reported and I understood at the time that I left that ferry boat--left the slip where the ferry boat was, that it had to be reported and I had full intention of reporting it, and I mentioned to Gargan and Markham something like, "You take care of the girls, I will take care of the accident." That is what I said and I dove into the water.

Now, I started to swim out into that tide and the tide suddenly became, felt an extraordinary shove and almost pulling me down again, the water pulling me down, and suddenly I realized at that time even as I failed to realize before I dove into the water that I was in a weakened condition, although as I had looked over that distance between the ferry slip and the other side, it seemed to me an inconsequential swim; but the water got colder, the tide began to draw me out and for the second time that evening I knew I was going to drown and the strength continued to leave me. By this time I was probably 50 yards off the shore and I remembered being swept down toward the direction of the Edgartown Light and well out into the darkness, and I continued to swim, tried to swim at a slower pace to be able to regain whatever kind of strength that was left in me.

And some time after, I think it was about the middle of the channel, a little further than that, the tide was much calmer, gentler, and I began to get my--make some progress, and finally was able to reach the other shore and all the nightmares and all the tragedy and all the loss of Mary Jo's death was right before me again. And when I was able to gain this shore, this Edgartown side, I pulled myself on the beach and then attempted to gain some strength. After that, I walked up one of the streets in the direction of the Shiretown Inn.

By walking up one of the streets, I walked into a parking lot that was adjacent to the Inn and I can remember almost having no further strength to continue, and leaning against a tree for a length of time, walking through the parking lot, trying to really gather some kind of idea as to what happened and feeling that I just had to go to my room at that time, which I did by walking through the front entrance of the Shiretown Inn up the stairs. [Q]

Q: Do you have any idea what time you arrived at the Shiretown Inn?
A: I would say some time before 2:00.
Q: Did you talk to anyone at that time?
A: I went to my room and I was shaking with chill. I took off all my clothes and collapsed on the bed. And at this time I was very conscious of a throbbing headache, of pains in my neck, of strain on my back; but what I was even more conscious of is the tragedy and loss of a very devoted friend.
Q: Now, did you change your clothing?

A: I was unable really to determine, detect the amount of time, and I could hear noise that was taking place. It seemed around me, on top of me, almost in the room, and after a period of time I wasn't sure whether it was morning or afternoon or nighttime,[18]/ and I put on--and I wanted to find out and I put on some dry clothes that were there, a pants and a shirt, and I opened the door and I saw what I believed to be a tourist or someone standing under the light off the balcony and asked what time it was. He mentioned to me it was, I think, 2:30, and went back into the room. [R]

Q: Had you known Miss Kopechne prior to July 18th?

A: Well, I have known her--my family has known her for a number of years. She has visited my house, my wife. She has visited Mrs. Robert Kennedy's house. She worked in the Robert Kennedy Presidential campaign, and I would say that we have known her for a number of years.

Q: Now, directing your--

A: If the question is, have I ever been out with Mary Jo--

Q: No, the question was whether you just knew her socially prior to this event.

A: Well, could I give you a fuller explanation, your Honor?

THE COURT: Go ahead.

THE WITNESS: I have never in my life, as I have stated in my television, had any personal relationship whatsoever with Mary Jo Kopechne. I never in my life have been either out with Mary Jo Kopechne nor have I ever been with her prior to that occasion where we were not in a general assemblage of friends, associates, or members of our family.

Q: Directing your attention to the 19th, at around 7:30 a.m., did you meet anyone at your room?

A: Not at 7:30 a.m.

Q: Did you meet anyone at anytime that morning at your room?

A: If your Honor would permit me to give--I would like to be specifically responsive, and I can, I think. It might be misleading to the Court if I just gave a specific response to it. Whatever the Court wants.

Q: Well, what time did you get up that morning?

A: I never really went to bed that night.[19]/

Q: After that noise at 2:30 in the morning, when did you first meet anyone?

A: Sometime after 8:00 I met the woman that was behind the counter at the Shiretown Inn and I met Mr. Richards and Mr. Moore, very briefly Mrs. Richards, and Mr. Gargan and Mr. Markham, and I saw Mr. Tretter, but to be specifically responsive as to who I met in my room, which I believe was the earlier question, was Mr. Markham and Mr. Gargan.

Q: Now, what time did Mr. Markham and Mr. Gargan arrive?

A: About a few-- I would think about 8:30.

Q: Did you have any conversation with (them) at that time?

18/ Two or three hours earlier he had been chiefly concerned with how dark it was. Darkness at noon?

19/ No; there are indications that we shall soon see that he spent a good part of it telephoning. Also, see discussion of Anomaly R.

A: Yes. They asked had I reported the accident, and why I hadn't reported the accident; and I told them about my own thoughts and feelings as I swam across that channel and how I was always willed that Mary Jo still lived; how I was hopeful even as that night went on and as I almost tossed and turned (?--Auth.), paced that room and walked around that room that night that somehow when they arrived in the morning that they were going to say that Mary Jo was still alive. I told them how I somehow believed that when the sun came up and it was a new morning that what had happened the night before would not have happened and did not happen, and how I just couldn't gain the strength within me, the moral strength, to call Mrs. Kopechne at 2:00 o'clock in the morning and tell her that her daughter was dead.[20]

Q: Now, at some time you actually did call Mrs. Kopechne?
A: Yes, I did.
Q: And prior to calling Mrs. Kopechne, did you cross over on the Chappaquiddick ferry to Chappaquiddick Island?
A: Yes, I did.
Q: And was Mr. Markham and Mr. Gargan with you?
A: Yes, they were.
Q: Now, did you then return to Edgartown?
A: Yes, I did.
Q: Did anything prompt or cause you to return to Edgartown?
A: Well, what do you mean by "prompt"?
Q: Well, did anything cause you to return?
A: Other than the intention of reporting the accident, the intention of which had been made earlier that morning. [S]
Q: But you didn't go directly from your room to the police department?
A: No, I did not.
Q: Did you have a particular reason for going to Chappaquiddick first?
A: Yes, it was to make a private phone call to one of the dearest and oldest friends that I have and that was to Mr. Burke Marshall. I didn't feel that I could use the phone that was available, the public phone that was available outside of the dining room at the Shiretown Inn, and it was my thought that once that I went to the police station, that I would be involved in a myriad of details and I wanted to talk to this friend before I undertook that responsibility.[21]
Q: You mean that--
THE COURT: Excuse me, Mr. Dinis, I think we will take the noon luncheon recess.[22]

---

[20] Once again, how or why was he so certain that Mary Jo was dead? People have been known to survive for several hours in submerged cars, breathing in air bubbles, and it is known that Mary Jo lived for a while thusly. And was it lack of moral strength that kept him from calling for professional help while, hopefully, there was still time?
Note: This reply of the Senator's is faithful to the text in The Inquest.

[21] According to Jack Olsen, in The Bridge at Chappaquiddick, Mr. Kennedy could have had his choice of a dozen public phones within two blocks of the Inn.

[22] Unfortunately, we will never know what Mr. Dinis's question was.

(Mr. Dinis resumed the questioning and Senator Kennedy said he had not been successful in his attempt to reach Burke Marshall, that he then returned to Edgartown and went to the local police department, arriving "sometime before 10 a.m." and made a statement.)

Q: Now, I have in my hand what purports to be the statement that you made to Chief Arena at that time, and in this statement you say-- well, would you read it first, Senator?
A: Yes.
That is correct. (The text of the statement follows.)

(On July 18, 1969, at approximately 11:15 p.m. on Chappaquiddick, Martha's Vineyard, Mass. I was driving my car on Main Street, Chappaquiddick, on my way to get the ferry back to Edgartown. I was unfamiliar with the road and turned right onto the Dyke Road instead of bearing hard left on Main Street.

After proceeding for approximately one-half mile on Dyke Road, I descended a hill and came upon a narrow bridge. The car went off the side of the bridge. There was one passenger with me, Miss Mary Jo Kopechne, a former secretary of my brother Robert Kennedy.

The car turned over and sank into the water and landed with the roof resting on the bottom. I attempted to open the door and window of the car but have no recollection of how I got out of the car.

I came to the surface and then repeatedly dove down to the car in an attempt to see if the passenger was still in the car. I was unsuccessful in the attempt.

I was exhausted and in a state of shock. I recall walking back to where my friends were eating. There was a car parked in front of the cottage, and I climbed into the back seat. I then asked for someone to bring me back to Edgartown.23/ I remember walking around for a period of time and then going back to my hotel room.

When I fully realized what had happened this morning, I immediately notified the police.)

Q: Now, Senator, prior to the effort you made to contact Burke Marshall by phone, did you make any other phone calls?
A: I made one call after 8 o'clock in the morning from the public phone outside of the restaurant at the Shiretown Inn.
Q: One call?
A: That is all. [T]
Q: And to whom did you make this call?
A: Mr. Stephen Smith, the party that I felt would know the number.
Q: With regard to the statement that you made at the police sta-

---

23/ This request was elaborated on in his inquest testimony, but isn't it a pity the Chief did not ask him whom he asked, how he managed to do so under the circumstances, how he managed to get back to his hotel and whether any rescue attempt was made at that time?

tion, Senator, you ended up by saying, "When I fully realized what had happened this morning I immediately contacted the police." Now, is that in fact what you did?

THE COURT: Mr. Dinis, are you going to ask the statement be put in the record?

MR. DINIS: Yes, your Honor.

THE COURT: Mr. Kennedy already said this was a copy of the statement he made. He already testified as to all his movements. Now, won't you let the record speak for itself? [U]

MR. DINIS: All right, your Honor.

Q: I show you, Mr. Kennedy, what purports to be a copy of the televised broadcast which you made approximately a week after the accident. Would you read that statement and tell me whether or not that is an exact copy of what you said? 24/

A: (Complies) Yes.

After a quick reading of it, I would say that that is accurate.

Q: Now, Senator, in that televised broadcast, you said, "I instructed Gargan and Markham not to alarm Mary Jo's friends that night," is that correct?

A: That is correct.

Q: Can you tell the Court what prompted you to give this instruction?

A: I felt strongly that if those girls were notified that an accident had taken place and that Mary Jo had in fact drowned, which I became convinced of by the time that Markham and Gargan and I left the scene of the accident, that it would only be a matter of seconds before all of those girls, who were long and dear friends of Mary Jo's, to go to the scene of the accident and dive themselves and enter the water and with, I felt, a good chance that some serious mishap might have occurred to any one of them. [VII] 25/

MR. DINIS: I have no further questions of Mr. Kennedy.

MR. KENNEDY: Your Honor, could I talk to my counsel before being released, just on one point that I might like to address the bench on?

THE COURT: Go ahead.

(Off-the-record discussion between Mr. Kennedy and his lawyers.)

THE COURT: And I think we can put in the record this question: Why did you not seek further assistance after Mr. Markham and Mr. Gargan had exhausted their efforts in attempting to reach Mary Jo?

MR. KENNEDY: Because I was completely convinced at that time that no further help and assistance would do Mary Jo any more good. I realized that she must be drowned and still in the car at this time, and it appeared the question in my mind at that time was, what should be done about the accident. 26/

24/ See appendix.
25/ This response merits being set apart because of its thought content; hence, the lineal separation. Don't you agree?
26/ A weighty decision; nothing simple, like calling the police. Once again, "completely convinced" of her death and that she was still in the car.

But the immediately preceding was not the "one more point" Mr. Kennedy had in mind. Ever the cavalier, and reputed even to have been eager for the inquest from the beginning (and the four-month postponement as well?), the conscientious senator made the following statement, which concluded his overt participation in the inquest.

MR. KENNEDY: Since the alcoholic intake is relevant, there is one further question, your Honor, and although I haven't been asked it, I feel that in all frankness and for a <u>complete</u> record that it should be included as a part of the complete proceedings, and that is that during the course of the race that afternoon that there were two other members of my crew and I shared what would be two beers between us at different points in the race, and one other occasion in which there was some modest intake of alcohol would be after the race at the slip in which Ross Richards' boat was attached, moored, that I shared a beer with Mr. John Driscoll. The sum and substance of that beer would be, I think, less than a quarter of one, but I felt that for the <u>complete</u> record that at least the Court should at least be aware of these instances as well.

THE COURT: Anything more?
MR. KENNEDY: There is nothing further.
THE COURT: Anything further, Mr. Dinis?
MR. DINIS: No, your Honor.
THE COURT: All right, you are excused, subject to further recall.

(Discussion off the record.)

* * *

But Mr. Kennedy was not recalled ("An inquest is not a trial of anyone."). He went back to his seat in the Senate, where his colleague, the gentleman from Montana, the Honorable Mike Mansfield (Senate Majority Leader), welcomed him and told him that that was where he "belonged." At any rate, that is where a whopping majority of the voting citizens of the Commonwealth of Massachusetts returned him in the general elections the following November and it is where he is now, in early 1972.

Now, for a better and more compleat understanding of the foregoing testimony, it is respectfully suggested that the reader review same and then carefully peruse that which follows.

2.

THE PERJURIES
OF
EDWARD M. KENNEDY

When, in the course of human events, it becomes necessary for one person to charge another with perjury, a decent respect to the opinions of mankind requires that the accuser should declare the causes for making such accusations.

Here goes.

PERJURY No. 1 (p. 6)

After hedging, the Senator yielded to the persistence of Mr. Dinis and admitted that the front window on his side had been open. Shortly thereafter, in his account of events immediately following the plunge into the pond (p. 7), he stated, "I can remember...feeling along the side to see if the window was open and the window was closed." Then, in the middle of page 8, he again said it was open. Kennedy admirers may be moved to explain these several self-contradictions as merely evidence of understandable uncertainty of memory and that he had been merely "correcting himself." Indeed, Mr. Kennedy had evidently forgotten that in the statement given to Chief Arena the morning of July 19th, purportedly giving the basic facts of the "accident" and to which he attested as to accuracy (see page 17 herein), he said, "I attempted to open the door and window of the car...", thus clearly implying that the window was closed.

Scuba diver John Farrar testified that he found the front window on the driver's side open (The Inquest, pp. 78 and 80).

PERJURY No. 2 (p. 6)

Senator Kennedy stated he had been driving approximately 20 miles per hour. (This was supported by Inspector George W. Kennedy (no relation to the Senator, he claimed), supervisor of the Registry of Motor Vehicles in Oak Bluffs, at the other end of Martha's Vineyard, in his testimony, which will be examined later.)

At 20 miles per hour, the rate is slightly more than 29 feet per second. Further in his testimony (The Inquest, p. 80), John Farrar stated that he had made some measurements "...as to the position of the car from the point of impact, the height of fall and the height of the water. ... The measurements of the position of the car with relationship to the bridge and the marks I found to be a projectory (sic — trajectory?) or a distance from the point of impact to the car of approximately 36 feet and a drop of approximately eight feet. (The 36 feet) would be the point measured from approximately the middle between the two marks on the bridge to the perpendicular in front of the car." (Note: The "two marks on the bridge" were made on the rub rail by the wheels as the car went over--the right front wheel first, then the left. This was because of the angle of the bridge to the road.) The horizontal distance the automobile hurtled from the bridge, then, was 36 feet, which increases the estimated speed even of that of Inspector Kennedy, who was generous enough to allow for a ten per cent variance and estimated the speed, in his opinion, at "20-22 miles per hour."

But that isn't all there is to it. When it left the bridge, the car traveled through air; then it struck water, which reduced its speed and the distance it would have traveled otherwise before hitting the bottom of the pond. Had this further distance been only three feet, the speed must be adjusted to about 26-1/2 miles per hour, based on considerations taken into account thus far. We can fix this as the minimum speed thusly, that conjecture being accepted:

The vertical drop was eight feet, Mr. Farrar said, but the photograph of the bridge on page 121 of The Inquest at slack tide forces the conclusion that this was only to the water. There was another shy six feet to go through water, totalling 14 feet, probably less a few inches. Now then, from one of the first laws we learn in physics, the Law of Falling Bodies, we know that during the first second of fall the vertical distance traveled is 16 feet (if wind resistance is not a factor, and it certainly was not here). Had this been a dry gully, the time lapse during the fall would have been seven-eighths of a second. But the cushioning effect of the water that reduced the horizontal distance also offsets this time fragment, vertical momentum considered as well, so that we may reasonably conjecture that the time between bridge and pond bottom was within a negligible fraction of one second. Mr. Farrar's measured 36 feet and the additional subjunctive three, totalling 39, gives us the estimated 26-1/2 miles per hour, which is 39 feet per second.

In its totality, the problem is complex, aggravated by unavoidable inexact measurements. Still further comments and observations will be made in a subsequent section, where presentation will be more opportune.

PERJURY No. 3 (p. 7)

Mr. Kennedy stated that at no time after he turned onto the unpaved Dike Road had he realized he had made a "wrong turn" (until just the moment before going off the bridge). Yet, he admitted he knew the road from the cottage (where the cook-out was held) to the ferry was paved. He also admitted having become "generally aware sometime" while on Dike Road that it was unpaved. Accordingly, therefore, he had to know that he was not on the way to the ferry, which he said was his immediate destination.

See further discussion concerning both Dike Road and the bridge in a later section.

PERJURY No. 4 (p. 7)

The Senator relied strongly on darkness to support his alibi. First, it was "an extremely dark night", which prepares the unwary listener or (█)der to accept his claim (█) "pitch blackness" under water at that moment. Note his reference to it four times in the course of this portion of his narrative. The truth is that the headlights of the car remained on for a few minutes after the plunge and created quite a bit of underwater illumination, although necessarily diffused. Mr. Kennedy reveals this himself (and the Engineering Department of the Oldsmobile Division of General Motors confirms it) further on when he relates his alleged return to the car after having been swept some 30 or 40 feet downstream (see page 9 and Perjury No 6). This was how he distinguished the front of the car from the rear, he said! Further on (p. 13), he relates how the headlights of the Valiant illuminated everything sufficiently for him to "see exactly what was happening" (the diving by Mr. Gargan and Mr. Markham) and make suggestions. I do believe there would have been enough light to have permitted such visibility, as, from having swum in the waters at Martha's Vineyard, I know it is remarkably clear.

PERJURY No. 5 (p. 8)

In his earlier testimony (pp. 7-8), he insisted that he n... been upside down after the car ran off the bridge. If it did not turn over, how was this explained?

In the statement given to Chief Arena (see p. 17), it was stated, "The car turned over and sank into the water and landed with the roof resting on the bottom." Although unsigned, the Senator attested to its accuracy in his testimony.

PERJURY No. 6 (p. 9)

The tide changed (low) at approximately 11:30 a.m. on Saturday, July 19th, according to Mr. Farrar's testimony (The Inquest, p. 80), and which can be confirmed by those at the scene at the time. The tide oscillation is approximately every six hours. Therefore, it was low tide at approximately 11:30 p.m., when Mr. Kennedy alleges the accident occurred. Accordingly, there was no current at all. Even if the car did not run off the bridge until a few minutes after it was (alleged to have been) sighted by Mr. Look at 12:45 a.m., the current could not have been running as fast as described. The time of the accident has been firmly established as far as testimony is concerned, however, as approximately 11:30 p.m., since*every surviving member of the party who admits having been at the cottage when the Senator left has given from 11:15 to 11:30 as the time of his departure, and his sworn account is that he proceeded directly to the bridge from having made a "wrong turn." This could not have taken more than a few minutes. Then he spent fifteen minutes diving for Mary Jo (he said), another fifteen minutes recuperating (he said) and still another fifteen minutes returning by foot from the bridge to the cottage for assistance (he said), arriving there at approximately 12:15, which has also been corroborated by others in the party.

* almost

PERJURY No. 7 (p.)

Here are the questions and answers concerning the length of acquaintance with Mary Jo by the long and dear friends in their respective testimonies (The Inquest, pages as noted).

Miss Esther Newburgh (p. 96):

> THE COURT: How long had you known Miss Kopechne?
> THE WITNESS: Since 1967.

Miss Ann Lyons (p. 112):

> Q: How long did you live with Mary Jo?
> A: Three years.

Miss Rosemary Keough (p. 115):

> Q: How long had you known Mary Jo Kopechne?
> A: I came to Senator Robert Kennedy's office September of 1967 and I have known her since then.

Miss Susan Tannenbaum (p. 118):

> Q: How long had you known Mary Jo?
> A: Approximately a year.

Miss Maryellen Lyons:

> This Miss Lyons was not asked the question.

Miss Keough had known Miss Kopechne less than two years, and we do not know if "since 1967" (for Miss Newburgh) means more or less than two years, but let us say the total for these two was forty-eight months.

If we consider only the three years Miss Ann Lyons shared the Washington apartment with Mary Jo and the "approximately a year" for Miss Tannenbaum (which could have been less than twelve months), the total for these two is another forty-eight months and the total for all four is ninety-six months, or an average of only twenty-four months acquaintance. Adding as much as a year to Miss Ann Lyons' acquaintance to allow for possible previous acquaintance brings the average to only twenty-seven months. By everyday standards, the length of acquaintance for any one of them is hardly a "long time".

3.

THE ANOMALIES
OF
EDWARD M. KENNEDY

Choosing a title for this section wasn't as easy as one might think. Many of the referenced statements were in all probability as perjurious as those in the preceding section, but sufficient absolute proof is lacking to warrant making such an outright charge, or some kind of defense is conjecturable, as sober reflection on the various circumstances will show. For most of them, quasi-perjuries might be accurate enough, but it was the definition given in a leading modern dictionary for the word, "anomaly", that decided the matter: Deviation from the normal or common order, form, or rule; abnormality.

That definition accepted, the reader may already have decided that the inquest, itself, was rather anomalous.

ANOMALY A (p. 5)

Mr. Kennedy said no one else was in the car with him but Miss Kopechne. Note the following excerpted testimony of Police Chief Arena (The Inquest, p. 85).

(Mr. Arena was describing a telephone conversation with the Senator, who was at Police Headquarters, the Chief having telephoned from the Malm house after having left the Dike Bridge Saturday morning after the recovery of Miss Kopechne's body.)

THE CHIEF: ...I said words to the effect that "I am sorry, I have some bad news. Your car was in an accident over here and the young lady is dead." He said, "I know."
I said, "Can you tell me was there anybody else in the car?"
He said, "Yes."
I said, "Are they in the water?"
He said, "No."

Since no one else heard both sides of the conversation, Mr. Kennedy's battalion of advisors[1] could accuse Chief Arena of falsifying—one word against another—or they might even railroad him into that federal mental hospital-prison[2] in Springfield, Missouri, if Mr. Arena insisted on his version. On the other hand, they could offer the explanation that what the Senator had really meant was, "Yes, I can tell you if there was anybody else in the car. No, there wasn't." If the reader wishes to believe this,.

---

[1] See Teddy Bare, pp. 43-44.
[2] If the reader's interest is aroused, see Destroy the Accuser, (Freedom Press Publ. Co. P.O. Box 462, Allapattah Sta., Miami, Fla., or order from Council for Statehood, P.O. Box 1121, No. Miami, Fla.) in which former Attorney General Robert Kennedy played a prominent role.

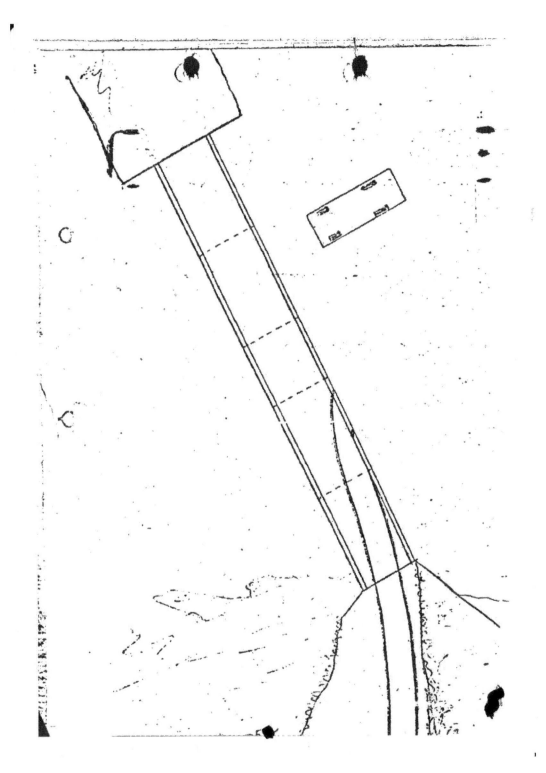

however, read on, re(...)on, read on and on and o(...). and ponder on Anomaly C.

ANOMALY B (p. 6)

The Senator said Mary Jo had been in the front seat; yet, in his emotion-packed narrative of the events following the alleged unsuccessful rescue attempts, he declared his belief that she was in the back of the car. In fact, as Zad Rust was also observant enough to note in Teddy Bare (p.223) that is just where she was found! (See bottom of page 13, herein.)

ANOMALY C (p. 6)

This is most unusual. Note the stipulation that there was nothing (to his knowledge) on the back seat at that particular time. Why the qualification? To be sure, there must have been times when another person or object had been on the back seat. As with virtually every other survivor of the party, Mr. Kennedy's memory regarding seemingly inconsequential detail was often unreliable, but not this time! He had evidently read Deputy Sheriff Christopher Look's account of having seen an automobile strikingly similar to the Oldsmobile at the junction of Chappaquiddick Road, referred to as "Main Street" by the Senator, and Dike Road (where the Senator should have made a left turn to reach the ferry but turned right instead) an hour and a half after the Senator said he left the cottage.

The Sheriff's account was totally unacceptable to Mr. Kennedy, of course, as Mr. Look had been positive that this was the same car he had seen pulled from the pond the next morning, complete with the beginning letter and the first and last digit of the license number he managed to note mentally-- L 7 - - - 7. This is also the probable reason for Mr. Kennedy's answering pertinent questions in advance almost immediately following this statement about not stopping, backing up or driving into Cemetery Road. Salient portions of Deputy Sheriff Look's testimony ran thusly:2a/

> A: I noticed it was a dark car that passed in front of me.
> Q: Where did it go when it passed in front of you?
> A: It went into a little dirt road maybe ten feet off the road that is commonly known, I believe, as Cemetery Road, and it stopped and as it stopped I proceeded around the corner and looked into the mirror of my car and noticed the car started to back up.
>
> ...
>
> A: When the automobile passed in front of me and also when I was walking towards it, there appeared to be a man driving and a woman in the front right-hand side and also either another person or an object of clothing, a handbag or something, sitting on the back.

2a/ The Inquest, p. 73.

ANOMALY D (p. 7)

This was a fantastic feat of memory! He remembered the car "just beginning" to go off the bridge, but was uncertain about applying the brakes -- "perhaps" a fraction of a second before--

Now let us revert to Perjury No. 2 and look further into the testimony of Inspector George Kennedy. By his own estimate, the Inspector arrived at the bridge that morning at about 10:30 and noticed some "skid marks" on the bridge "starting at the edge of the bridge on the dirt." There were numerous mentionings of the skid marks, which, for some unclear reason, he seemed to imply were easier both to detect and measure on the wooden bridge than on the all-gravel approach. That there had been actual braking, however, does not appear to have been firmly and incontestably established, although Judge Boyle seemed to think so in his Report. In a contradictory vein, in The Bridge at Chappaquiddick (p. 257), Jack Olsen tells us that the "skid marks" were so light that no rubber residue was left and that accident experts who examined the area later were uncertain whether the brakes had been fully activated. Also anomalously, in the August 1, 1969 cover story, Time (p. 12, and of which the frequently quoted Mr. Olsen is a senior editor, remember) says there were no skid marks.

Now let us approach the matter of the Inspector's estimate of 20-22 miles per hour as the speed of the Oldsmobile on its take-off run. Assistant District Attorney Armand Fernandes examined Inspector Kennedy. The following excerpt has been slightly abridged to relieve the reader of irrelevancies.[2b/]

Q: ...drawing on your experience and based on the physical evidence, are you able to form an opinion--and I want a yes or no answer--
A: I would say yes.
THE COURT: Wait a minute. He hasn't asked you as to what.
Q: --as to what speed a car would be traveling in order to leave the skid marks which you described for the Court?
A: Yes.
Q: Could you tell us what your opinion was?
A: Approximately 20 to 22 miles per hour.
Q: And how do you base that--?
A: All right, a car operating at 20 miles per hour has a reaction time of any person operating approximately three-quarters of a second before a person removes his foot from the gas and applies the brake. Approximately at 20 miles an hour the vehicle would move approximately 22 feet in the three-quarters of a second for the reaction time. Then a vehicle, after the brakes have been applied, should stop in 25 feet. Now, there is a distance of 25, 22 -- 47 feet.
THE COURT: Well, I'm going to stop you there now...I don't know...

Neither does anyone else know, Judge.
Surprisingly enough, however, instead of His Honor asking how the Inspector had determined that the car had actually stopped with-

─────────
[2b/] Ibid., p. 68.

in the 47 feet from the beginning of the "reaction time" required for validity, the questions that followed concerned the weight of the car, condition of the tires and brakes (both excellent), etc. At no time was this fact established.

Inspector Kennedy also made some measurements—the "skid marks", the distances from the edge of the bridge to the points where the wheels went over. The right one was 18 feet, the left, 33 feet, two inches. But an extremely interesting thing about the locations of those points of departure from the bridge that the Inspector did not reveal is that the one made by the left wheel ended less than four feet from the "peak" of the bridge. This will be more clearly understood from a superficial description of the bridge construction in Anomaly G. Suffice it to say here that there is an elevated center section and that the ramp sections on either side have a gradient of some eleven degrees or more. What this means is that the vehicle ran 15 feet up an eleven-degree inclined plane before plunging off and that this would have had a decelerating effect, which means further that the estimated speed of 26-1/2 miles per hour when the car hit the edge of the bridge is due another upgrading. How about 28?

Here is some more. On each side of the bridge there is a low curb or rub rail nine inches wide and there was a deep gouge at the approximate midpoint between the two tire marks caused by the transmission housing as it went over. From the standpoint of horizontally directed force, as when the transmission housing gashed across it, the width is equivalent to thickness. This caused more deceleration, of course, and so more speed upgrading is necessary. To 30?

But we aren't finished yet. If the brakes were applied, as Inspector Kennedy indicated, this would mean more deceleration from the beginning of the bridge. The Inspector stated, and rightly so, that it takes a greater distance to stop on wood than on macadam and still more if the surface is lightly sandy. The mentioned 25 feet was for macadam. One of the pieces of defensive evidence submitted on Senator Kennedy's behalf was a rather sophisticated engineering study, mentioned more fully in Anomaly G, that included several one-the-scene tests made following the accident. Here is an excerpt:2bb/

> Data on a test performed in the presence of Mr. George Kennedy, of the Massachusetts Division of Motor Vehicles, in which a 1969 Chevrolet approached the bridge at 20 mph. The brakes were applied at the instant the front wheels touched the bridge. The car came to a stop with the front wheels at a distance of 33 feet from the beginning of the bridge. The test was performed on a dry bridge, but with a slightly sandy surface.

That was just two inches short of where the left front wheel of the Oldsmobile went off, wasn't it? Accordingly, if the 1967 Oldsmobile was traveling at only 20-22 miles per hour as it approached the bridge, as both Senator Kennedy and Inspector Kennedy maintained, it should have at least decelerated sufficiently that, if it did not stop completely, only the right front wheel would have gone over. But did it? You know it didn't. The flight of the Oldsmobile ended 36 feet further east on the bottom of the neck just entering into Poucha Pond. And so we are now faced with more necessary speed upgrading. 35? 40? 45? 50?

We do not know why Inspector Kennedy obviously ignored this greater distance, since he said the car had been moved from its original spot at the time of his arrival, but we do know from his testimony that the Senator knew that the Inspector knew about the plunge. From the bridge, the Inspector went directly to Police Headquarters, where the Senator was at the time and spent about forty-five minutes with him. But Inspector Kennedy is an honorable man; so are they all, all, honorable men (and women).

Now, what was that Judge Boyle said at the opening just two days before Inspector Kennedy testified?

2bb/ Ibid., p. 93.

"It is the duty of the Court to seek out and receive any and all information and testimony which is relevant, pertinent and material to the question as to whether criminal conduct caused or contributed to the death..."

Just what the Inspector expected to accomplish with the injection of the "reaction time" factor is also unclear or what bearing it has. Moreover, I am inclined to believe that three-quarters of a second is more than generous--in other words, a l o n g time--for a man only 37 years of age, in good physical condition and mentally alert. When drunk? That's different, but the Senator swore he was cold sober.

And if we may revert to the upwardly adjusted estimated speed at which the Senator and Mary Jo may have been traveling, this puts the report of the two Malm ladies, mother and daughter, who were living in the "Dyke House" (estimated from only 100 to 150 yards from the bridge) in a slightly different key. Both told Chief Arena (The Inquest, p. 87) they had heard a car going past unusually fast toward the bridge some time between 11:15 and 11:45 p.m., although their accounts did not coincide exactly in every detail. What puts it a little off-key is that the time is a minimum of one hour too early to meld with Deputy Sheriff Look report. But isn't it a pity the Malms couldn't have testified in person?

ANOMALY E (p. 7)

Why was he so sure no one would be looking for them until morning? Should he not have assumed that the others would have returned to Edgartown as planned? And would Miss Newburgh (Mary Jo's roommate at the motel) not have missed her when she returned? And would Mr. Gargan (who shared Mr. Kennedy's room at the Shiretown Inn) not have missed him? Would the normal reaction not have been to inform at least some of the others and, both having been discovered missing, go look for them and/or notify the police?

ANOMALY F (p. 8)

Had he really been upside down, with no seat belt holding him (none was mentioned), all his weight would necessarily have been on his head, since he was obviously using his hands to try to hold the water back, and there was no mention of this uncomfortable position. The contusion on top of his head and the minor neck injury attested to by a physician by affidavit does not necessarily confirm that he did land on his head.

ANOMALY G (p. 9)

The Senator's implication is clear that he did not see the

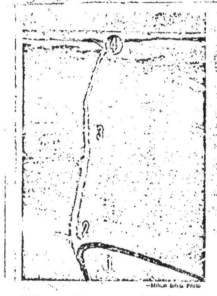

Scene of tragedy on Chappaquiddick. (1) The blacktop road along which Senator Kennedy drove with Miss Kopechne as his passenger. (2) Where Kennedy said he intended to turn left to follow the blacktop road to the Edgartown ferry. Instead, he turned right onto (3) Dyke Road, a sandy lane that leads to (4) Dyke Bridge, from which the Kennedy car plunged into the tidal pond at the right.

P. 30   U.S. NEWS & WORLD REPORT, Sept. 15, 1969

Aug. 1, 1969.   APPROACH TO DIKE BRIDGE AS ILLUMINATED BY AUTO HEADLIGHTS

bridge until he was practically on it for the simple reason that he didn't know it was there, despite having been over it twice that day. The argument here could well be that "someone else had been driving" and he just hadn't paid any attention to the local scenery, which held no novelty for him. This argument might win credence from some and prove difficult to dispute if the Dike Bridge was an ordinary one, but it isn't; it is extraordinary and the extraordinary, the anomalous, attracts attention.

Author Olsen tells us more than once in The Bridge at Chappaquiddick (e.g., pp. 116 and 135), that it is clearly visible from the road from a distance of 200 yards or more, partly due to its angle to the road. As if the rather abrupt change in scenery wasn't enough to attract attention (the trees and brush lining the road stop before reaching the Malm house), the road becomes increasingly rough, with ruts and a couple of pot holes not far from the westerly end of the bridge that cause any normal driver to slow down, bridge or not. And it is reasonable to assume that Mr. Crimmins is a normal driver. Then there is the unusual 27-degree angle of the bridge to the road (according to Inspector George Kennedy) and then the narrowness of the bridge, itself—only ten feet, six inches wide—to command the attention. (The cited article in Time (p. 12, Aug. 1, 1969) says the local residents recommend coming to a full stop before going onto the bridge, then inching forward at a respectable 5 m.p.h. until safely on the other side.)

But these, other than the width, are only the approach factors; there is the bridge, itself. Most rural bridges are essentially level with the road and it is, indeed, possible to zip past them without notice; but not the Dike. It is "humpbacked", and this contributes mostly to its visibility from a distance. In an elaborate report in the form of an affidavit by professional engineer Eugene D. Jones, Vice President in charge of the New England Division of Frederic R. Harris, Inc., Consulting Engineers, the bridge is described as having a center span 11'-9" long. Let's say twelve feet. Then it says this span varies in clearance from three feet to five feet above the water. It does not say, however, whether this variance is due to the tide or if it refers to the levels of the center approach sections to the said center span. Looking a various photographs of the bridge, it is easy to believe the reference is to the bridge, itself. These approach sections appear to be between 15 and 20 feet long and rise, ramplike, to meet each respective end of the elevated center span. This is why it is known locally as "the hump". The center span looks as if it is easily two feet above the beginning of each approaching ramp section, which would give the ramps a gradient of no less than ten degrees, and going over it the first time in an automobile, whether driving or as a passenger, must be quite an experience. With a wheelbase of ten feet, four inches (according to the manufacturer) and a minimum clearance of just about six inches, Mr. Crimmins must have had some misgivings before reaching the other side and quite possibly some conversation with the Senator as to whether to risk it! For example, read the following excerpt (slightly abridged) from Mr. Crimmins' testimony and see if you agree.[2c/]

[2c/] Ibid., p. 49.

THE COURT: Did you drive (the Senator) to the beach?
THE WITNESS: Yes, Your Honor.
THE COURT: Did you drive him over the Dike Bridge?
THE WITNESS: Yes, I did.
THE COURT: Did you have any difficulty negotiating it?
THE WITNESS: Just the hump.
THE COURT: And you brought the car back over the bridge?
THE WITNESS: Yes, sir.
THE COURT: And is that an Oldsmobile Model 88?
THE WITNESS: Yes, sir.

Now, why not consider a few noteworthy things about this bit of information? For instance, Mr. Crimmins' use of the colloquial term, "the hump", regarding the bridge and that His Honor did not have to ask what he meant by it. In fact, acquaintance with it was indicated by his apparent anticipation of difficulty. Also, Mr. Crimmins was not asked whether this was his first visit to Chappaquiddick Island, but Mr. Kennedy claimed it was his. Mr. Crimmins arrived on Martha's Vineyard on Wednesday, the 16th, and spent that night alone at the cottage. Messrs. Gargan, Markham and LaRosa arrived the next afternoon and evening, but spent the night at the Shiretown Inn. The next day, Friday, the 18th, Mr. Crimmins met the Senator at the local airport and, as we k... from the Senator's testimony, drove him to the cottage, then to the beach. Instead of remaining at the beach, however, Mr. Crimmins then went to the Shiretown Inn and drove the Senator back to the cottage that evening after the race. The point here is that there was little opportunity for him to learn such a term for such a remote and obscure structure as the Dike Bridge. Of course, Mr. Crimmins could well have visited the island previously, but he gave his residence as South Boston, his occupation as legal aide and investigator, and part-time chauffeur (evenings and weekends) for the Senator when the latter is in the Boston area, having enjoyed this relationship for nine years. Where did he get the familiarity?

And then, there is the unmistakable and almost inimitable sound made when driving over a wooden bridge of this type, accentuated by "the hump", which is concave on the undersurface, of course, and which probably amplifies and deepens the tone.

Back to the Jones report, it even includes the results of a survey of Dike Road. To the uninitiated, technical terminology descriptive of the simplest thing can sometimes be almost overwhelming. Here, for example, is the way the licensed surveyors described it, in part: "...the roadway is on tangent for approximately 225'...then curves to the right on a radius of 900' for approximately 51'. From the end of this curve, the roadway continues on tangent for approximately 263' to Station 5+40. From this point, the alignment of the roadway is a series of three (3) closely connected curves as it approaches the bridge." Rather than being a good layout for part of an amusement park ride or a proving ground course, a quick glance at the aerial photo of Dike Road on page 30, U.S. News & World Report, Sept. 15, 1969, will show the curves to be very gentle. In fact, except for possibly the last

Erratum

The excerpts on this page (32) were erroneously ascribed to the Jones Report. Actually, they are from still another report prepared by Donald L. Sullivan, of the Arthur D. Little Company. It is in the same section of The Inquest as the Jones Report.

150 feet, it would prob( ) be a good place for beginners learning to drive. Here are a few more excerpts from this ( )ly professional and technical study and report (pp. 92-95, The Inquest).

Approaching the bridge, the road is straight for at least 3/10 of a mile, except for the last 150 feet. A 1% downgrade extends from 630 feet to within 100 feet of the bridge. (Note: A 1% downgrade is practically level and this is probably the "hill" referred to in the statement given to Chief Arena, page 17.*) Vegetation on the right at a distance of about 120 feet from the bridge forces one to turn to the left, so that highbeam headlights do not illuminate the bridge <u>at this point</u>. Just as one turns back to the right at between 90' and 30' from the bridge, one's lights are deflected sharply upward so that <u>again the bridge is not illuminated</u>. The rapid right turn, left turn, and sharp upward deflection are not only distracting but also make it difficult to see the bridge before one is on it.

Sounds gruesome, doesn't it? What this report does <u>not</u> reveal (in The Inquest) is the approximate point in distance from which the bridge is <u>first</u> illuminated when driving at night and becomes visible. Neither does it reveal that the road widens perceptibly well before reaching the Malm house and that the "closely connected curves" are actually very, very gentle S-curves, so gentle that they can be negotiated practically without turning the wheels by permitting the path of a vehicle to be almost straight and approach the left lane momentarily as it progresses, the roadway turning slightly to the right, thus keeping the bridge in view. Thus it is, too, with the "vegetation on the right" that "forces" a turn to the left. It is part of a smaller, but also gentle, S-curve. In other words, the rapid turns are necessitated <u>only</u> if the driver hugs the right side of this little-traveled road, and the losses of view of the bridge resulting therefrom are only momentary. Yes, to be sure, this is "driving by the book" and is technically correct, but any normal, experienced driver, especially when driving on an unpaved country road with no lane markings, and when it is obvious that no risk exists with respect to another oncoming vehicle, will permit his car to ease from one side to the other to straighten out gentle curves. But here is some more--

The motion picture (Yes!--Auth.) shows that the bridge is visible for a period of less than three seconds prior to the accident if the car approached the bridge at 20 miles per hour.

The series of still pictures shows that at distances in excess of 100 feet from the bridge that the high-beam headlights strike the ground for a long period of time well in front of and to the left of the bridge. Just as the headlights come right, toward the bridge, at a distance of between 100 feet and 50 feet, the headlights are tipped up sharply by the rising terrain.

There is even more of such description and, if one is not

* --Auth.

swept away on a wave of sympathy for the Senator, one is forced to ask a few questions. As a starter, with such horrendous terrain (surely, the Senator must have realized there was nothing like this on the paved road between the cook-out cottage and the ferry!) what normal driver would not drastically reduce speed? Did Mr. Crimmins do so? Incidentally, that cited photo in Time clearly shows the probable "rising terrain" as a bump that extends pretty much all the way across the road, unless what was meant in everyday language as a "dip". Mr. Jones and his party evidently missed this photo (how did the Senator miss it?)--but Mr. Jones, also, is an honorable man; so are they all, all, honorable men (and women).

And then there was Mary Jo, who had been over the route to and from the ferry not just twice that day (as had the Senator), but five times. Did she notice nothing anomalous about going down Dike Road? If she did, did she mention it to the Senator? And if she did, did the Senator pay no attention? Did it not jog his own memory?

And what about the ~~matter-of-a~~ warning sign on the roadside prior to reaching the junction with Dike Road, with an arrow and the words "To the Ferry" in reflector-type illumination? (This was not mentioned in the inquest.)

Less than three seconds' visibility, did he say? All right, two and three-quarters. So we deduct an excessively long three-quarters of a second for reaction time (according to Inspector Kennedy) and we have two seconds left, or 59.8 feet from the edge of the bridge. Shall we say 60? Now, the 25 feet the Inspector had given for stopping at 20 miles per hour was on dry macadam and, a little later in his testimony, he said "On wood, the car would travel much farther." This is believable. In fact, part of the study conducted by Mr. Jones included the testing of a 1969 Chevrolet at Dike Bridge in September 1969, when it required 33 feet to stop, the brakes having been applied the moment the front wheels touched the bridge traveling at 20 miles per hour. (He even got the Inspector and the Chief in the act, the brake testing being done in the presence of the former, with the latter clocking the speeds.) This still leaves 27 feet of bumpy Dike Road, plus the 18 feet from the edge of the bridge to the point on the right rub rail where he went over, making 45 feet of roadway and bridge between the vehicle and Poucha Pond after reaction time and expanded stopping distance, during which it is uncertain whether Mr. Kennedy (the Senator, that is) actually applied his brakes.

This was an expensive report, undertaken, Mr. Jones said, at the request of Ropes & Gray, Attorneys at Law. Need we ask who requested Ropes & Gray, Esqs., to request Frederic R. Harris, Inc., Consulting Engineers, to make the study? According to a statement in the introductory portion of the exhibit, the inspection of the road and bridge was made on December 29 and 30, 1969, just a week before the inquest. Why?. Did the Senator think the residents of Martha's Vineyard were unaware of the condition of the road and bridge, or was he afraid it might go further and be the concern of others lacking first-hand familiarity? It did.

ANOMALY H (p. 9)

As in Anomaly D, he remembered "just beginning" to go off the bridge, but could not be positive about turning his wheels. Let's see what else Inspector Kennedy said about the "skid marks". 2d/

A: When I arrived at the scene I observed a car in the water on the right side of the bridge. I had noticed skid marks on the bridge starting at the edge of the bridge on the dirt and continuing straight to the right and over.

Paraphrasing the description of the tire marks in The Bridge at Chappaquiddick, it was as if the wheels had been "locked in position." And with an acknowledged minimum of almost three seconds visibility time? I submit that "reaction time" for turning wheels is appreciably less than that for braking. But what was that the Judge said in his report about the turn onto Dike Road?

I infer...that Kennedy did not intend to drive to the ferry slip and his turn onto Dike Road was intentional. ... I believe it probable that Kennedy knew of the hazard that lay ahead of him on Dike Road, but that, for some reason not apparent from the testimony, he failed to exercise due care as he approached the bridge.

ANOMALY J (p. 9)

One may well ask what kind of response Judge Boyle could possibly have expected to such a question. However, it is rumored that the popular opinion in and around Edgartown is that Mr. Kennedy waited as long as he did to report to the police because he was very drunk. This, of course, would have been obvious to another person. And then there would have been an incriminating "breath test" to be feared if this was true. However, there is yet another possible reason for the delay. Please be patient.

ANOMALY K (p. 10)

The Senator said he couldn't swim because of the current, so he swam to where he could wade. That was really a good trick and it indicates tremendous resourcefulness. However, Perjury No. 6 puts the tale of the attempted rescue in a different light. See also Perjury No. 4.

ANOMALY L (p. 10)

Now the Senator is absolutely right! The bridge does run almost east-west. In the course of preparing this material, I examined a rather large-scale map of Chappaquiddick Island that was prepared by the U.S. Coast & Geodetic Survey that also shows

---

2d/ Ibid., p. 66.

compass directions by degrees. Believe it or not, it even shows Dike Road and the bridge. I would bet that a line from the center of the road from Wrong-Turn Junction to the beginning of the bridge (the road is almost straight) would have a bearing of very nearly 120 degrees. Now then, if we subtract Inspector Kennedy's 27 degrees for the angle of the bridge to the road we get 93 degrees, which is almost due east (90 degrees). (The map is in slight error; it shows the bridge at an angle to the road on the easterly side of the cut, rather than the westerly.)

Supportive to this is the introductory phrase preceding the first quotation from civil engineer Eugene Jones's report given on page 31: "Starting at Station 0+00 and proceeding in a southeasterly direction, the roadway is on tangent...etc." This does not necessarily mean <u>due</u> southeast, or a bearing of precisely 135 degrees, but in that general direction, which could be 120 degrees.

But what is anomalous about this? Why, simply that the Senator said (see page 4) he had never been on Chappaquiddick before the day of the swim and later cook-out, and such accuracy as to the lay of such a road and ramshackle bridge is unusual. Incidentally, the people around those parts thought such a statement was a little anomalous. Participating in the Edgartown Regatta, which he did that Friday afternoon (the race), has long been a family tradition, and in all that time he never visited Chappaquiddick.

ANOMALY M (p. 11)

It is a pity we don't know where "up to *this point*" was, but it is surmisable that it was somewhere on the upper part of his body, perhaps around his neck or chin. This is based on scuba diver Farrar's estimate of a depth of from six to seven feet in the immediate vicinity of the vehicle at approximately 8:45 a.m. when he recovered the body. Mr. Kennedy is reputed to be six feet, two inches, tall, and let us be mindful that it was a slack tide he had plunged into and the water, therefore, was lower than it had been at the approximate midpoint between tides, as with Mr. Farrar.

And if he had been truly unable to stand, as he claimed, how would he have been able to say "It was up to *this point*"?

ANOMALY N (p. 11)

Here are some excerpts from the testimony of Chief Arena:[2e/]

A: This (statement) is from Sylvia R. Malm. She is the mother of the family. "On Saturday morning, July 19, 1969, two boys knocked on my door and said there is a car upside-down in the water by the bridge. ...Sometime during the evening before, I was aware of a car going faster than usual going toward the Dike. I have no idea of the time. I think I went to sleep sometime between 11:30 and 12:00 midnight, but I do not know the time. I heard nothing during the night. ... <u>a night light was burning all night.</u>"

[2e/] Ibid., p. 87.

Then I have a statement from Sylvia A. Malm, who is the daughter. "On Friday night, July 18, 1969, I lay in bed underneath an open window which faces east (that is, the bridge.-- Auth.) from 11 p.m. to 12 midnight, looking at the clock just before I turned my light out."

Remembering how Senator Kennedy shouted Mary Jo's name (p. 9) and that the lights of the Valiant must have shone into Miss Malm's window when he returned with Messrs. Gargan and Markham to resume rescue operations, we must pause to regret that the Malms are such deep sleepers. But Chief Arena said, a little further on--

A: Yes, there is a house diagonally across the street on the right (occupied by a Mrs. Smith). I had a conversation with Mrs. Smith and she stated she had a night light in one of her children's rooms which she left on all night. This was on the road side of the house.

It is anomalous, too, that the Senator used the word, "cottage", whereas Mr. Dinis said "houses." The truth is, I believe, that the so-called Malm house is a cottage, which is to say, a small house, as are most houses on Chappaquiddick Island. In his report following the inquest, Judge Boyle referred to it thus: (The Inquest, p. 125): "A short distance before Dyke Bridge, there is a small house called 'Dyke House', then occupied by a Mrs. Malm and her daughter."

The significance of this is that there had been ample opportunity to observe both the Malm (or "Dyke") house and the Smith house twice the preceding day, going to and returning from the beach, especially the return, since there are no trees to obscure the vision between the bridge and the house. There was also an opportunity to observe one or more of these houses on the way to the bridge on that fatal drive, particularly if he was driving only 20 miles per hour.

Notice, also, still another attempt to clutch at the mask of night. Darkness is conceded. The crescent moon was below the horizon a full hour before the alleged time of the "accident". However, the eye adjusts to gradations of light, the pupils dilating with diminution of luminosity, and Mr. Kennedy had been exposed to this "pitch blackness" by his own reckoning a minimum of a half-hour. And bear in mind the absence of trees to obscure the starlight, faint as it is. (It was a clear night, remember? And he said he saw the "silhouettes" of the trees. Against what?)

ANOMALY O (p. 12)

Mr. Kennedy said that Mr. Gargan's arm was "all bruised and bloodied." Let's look at portions of the testimonies of just a few persons who saw Mr. Gargan the next morning. Richard P. Hewitt was the ferry operator who took our heroic trio to and from Chappaquiddick Island that Saturday morning and had this to say:[2f/]

[2f/] Ibid., p. 81.

Q: Do you recall whether or not any of them (Kennedy, Gargan or Markham) appeared to be injured in any way?
A: I didn't notice anything that would make me think that they were injured.

Mr. Gargan happened to be at the Police Station at the same time as Inspector Kennedy, who said this:2g/

Q: Were you in close proximity to Mr. Gargan?
A: I was.
Q: Did you have occasion to see his arms?
A: I did.
Q: Did you observe any marks?
A: I did not.
Q: Did you make any observations as to limping or any sign of injury to anyone?
A: No limping on anybody.

And Chief Arena had this to say:2h/

Q: In your observation of Mr. Kennedy (the Senator), did you make note of any injuries or bruises?
A: No physical injuries.
Q: To Mr. Markham?
A: No, sir.
Q: To Mr. Gargan?
A: No, sir.

In describing her activities Saturday morning at the cottage, Miss Newburgh said (having slept in the same room with Mr. Gargan and several others who considered themselves marooned):2j/

A: (Mr. Gargan) was walking out the door when I got up at 8 o'clock. I didn't talk to him. I just saw him for a few minutes. I saw him for five minutes when he picked me up in the car, another ten minutes in the cottage and I saw him later that morning.
Q: ...did you observe any injuries that he had received?
A: No.
Q: Was there mention by anyone that he had received injuries anywhere in any manner at that time?
A: No.

This anomaly could be defended on grounds of the way it had "seemed at the moment" when the Senator was purportedly in a "state of shock." On the other hand, let us remember that Mr. Kennedy said Mr. Gargan had managed to get half-way into the vehicle at one time, which Mr. Gargan later corroborated in his own testimony. And let us remember, also, that the windows of the car on the passenger's side were "blown out", which means that Mr. Gargan might well have cut one of his arms on the underside, for instance, on a fragment of glass. Such a cut could have been sufficient to produce visible bleeding, but slight enough to have escaped notice if covered by his shirt sleeve. Let us remember this bloodiness.

2g/ Ibid., p. 72; 2h/ Ibid., p. 86; 2j/ Ibid., p. 93.

ANOMALY P (p. 13)

This is, first, an extension of Anomaly B, preceding.
Next, if the reader wishes to avoid being swept away by a strong but artificially-generated current of sympathy, reviewing Perjuries No. 6 and 7 is recommended. Here, the Senator seems to be "borrowing" sympathy genuinely due Mrs. Kopechne and using it as a blind for his not having sought professional assistance, the explanation he gave for not doing so in his response footnoted 26, page 18, notwithstanding. In addition to several houses between the bridge and the ferry where assistance could have been summoned or obtained, there is a fire station (unmanned, but with a device for registering alarm) with a red light that burns all night) only a couple of hundred yards or so from the cook-out cottage toward the junction of the paved road with Dike Road.3/ For some reason, known or unknown, this was not brought out during the inquest, but it was known to the party. Miss Ann Lyons was one of a group that went for two walks along the road after the Senator and Mary Jo left and she said this about one of them: "...we walked well past the fire station on this particular walk." 4/ And, most ironically, the Chief of the Volunteer Fire Company lives almost right across the road, even nearer to the cottage, and he was home that night.5/ This was not mentioned in the inquest, either.
The reader will recognize the remainder of this response as part of the "sympathy current."
See also footnote 26, page 18.

ANOMALY Q (p. 14)

The sympathy current is still the theme of this portion of the yarn, the main stream being shifted back to well known human limitations, physical fatigue from "diving" and the inability to hold his breath being the Senator's principal complaints, with a reprise on his own life becoming endangered. Those who have reviewed Perjury No. 6, along with Anomaly M, are best prepared to withstand the onslaught and see the whole matter of the "diving" surrounded by a huge question mark.
As for the alleged swim, the channel at the ferry run is now sometimes referred to in and around Edgartown as "Teddy's credibility gap." It is narrow, yes, and the tidal current is reputed to be particularly ferocious, and many Martha's Vineyardites have serious doubts that he did it, good swimmer though he may be. Messrs. Gargan and Markham are not of that ilk, however, as we can see from their testimonies. Mr. Gargan first--6/

    Q: Now, when you saw the Senator jump into the channel there, did you see him reach the other side?
    A: I did not.
    Q: Weren't you concerned about his--

3/ Teddy Bare, p. 65.
4/ The Inquest, p. 108.
5/ Teddy Bare, p. 65.
6/ The Inquest, p. 36.

A: No.[7]
Q: --ability to make it?
A: No, not at all. The Senator can swim that five or six times both ways. That may seem unusual, Mr. Dinis, except I have been with the Senator 30 years swimming and sailing and I don't know if you know the breakwater off Hyannisport, but we used to swim every day around that, the breakwater, and it is the only thing the Senator has done since his back injury, besides skiing. The real form of exercise for the Senator since the back injury is swimming.

And now, Mr. Markham--[8]

Q: Were you concerned with the fact of whether or not (the Senator) would arrive safely on the other side?
A: No, I wasn't.

Let us note that this confidence was not dampened by their knowledge of Mr. Kennedy's (claimed) previous exhaustion, plus his having been clothed at least in a shirt and slacks, which would have offered some impediment, not to mention sneakers that can get quite heavy when filled with water (you can't keep it out, not even with your hands).

No doubt there are times, depending on varying factors, when that current is dangerously swift for a swimmer, even should he be Senator Kennedy. Whether it was so at approximately 1:30 a.m., which is within a few minutes of the time he alleges he made the swim, is subject to question, however. You see, they have funny water at Martha's Vineyard. It is funny in other ways than not being able to hold it back with your hands. Now, even a self-respecting Arizonian knows there are high and low tides (flood and ebb, if you want to be very nautical) at any place on the ocean. But that isn't enough at Edgartown; at times, at least, they have "double floods" and "double ebbs". This anomaly contributes to surface currents in that channel, which is considerably deeper than the one at Dike Bridge, being quite different from those, say, six or seven feet below the surface. Since the body is essentially horizontal when swimming, the surface currents are the ones the Senator had to worry about. Coincidentally, at the same place where the map of Chappaquiddick Island was inspected[9] they have a book published by the U.S. Department of Commerce entitled Current Tables, 1969, Atlantic Coast of North America, and it gives all kinds of information about ocean currents, including at Edgartown. It shows that at 0036 hours (1:36 a.m. EDST), when Senator Kennedy should have been in the water, the surface current was slack. (This is despite a high water time of 3:49 a.m., EDST.) No wonder Jared Grant, owner of the ferry and who was on duty the night of July 18th-19th, and who remained at the Edgartown ferry slip until 1:20, said in his testimony: "It was a beautiful night, very calm. The water was like glass."[10] The only way the subsurface current

---

[7] Remember Inspector Kennedy's eager response? Anomaly D, p. 27.
[8] The Inquest, p. 46.
[9] National Ocean Survey Administration, 30 Rockefeller Plaza, New York City.
[10] The Inquest, p. 83.

could have affected him would have been had he stopped swimming and treaded water so that his feet might have reached the tidal current. But treading water is just as fatiguing as swimming, and there was no mention of it, anyway. The classical maneuver tired swimmers resort to in order to rest is floating, which the Senator did mention in his response footnoted 12, page 11.

But for all the currents and tides in the affairs of Senator Kennedy, the ineluctable question arises: was the swim necessary?

It was not.

Mr. Grant, the ferry owner, had more to say.[11]

Q: Were you available for calls if someone wanted the ferry that night?
A: I was. Year round, we are on call 24 hours a day.
Q: And is there a public telephone that you are aware of also on Chappaquiddick?
A: Yes.
Q: When do you normally close down?
A: Usually, we close down at 12:00 (midnight).
Q: And if someone wanted you after 12, where would they call?
A: My house.
Q: If I am at Chappaquiddick and I want the ferry and you are not at the landing...If I use the telephone, where does this call get me, to your home?
A: Yes...there is a regular dial system and my number is posted.

Now then, if that trio didn't know the telephone was there, with the number plainly marked, what view should we take of the "private" phone call to the Senator's dear old friend, Burke Marshall, the next morning from Chappaquiddick? (See Anomaly S.)

"It is the duty of the Court to seek out and receive any and all information and testimony which is relevant, pertinent and material to the question as to whether criminal conduct caused or contributed to the death..."

Yes, Judge, thank you. You told us that in your opening remarks (page 1).

And so now perhaps we should revert to the skepticism about the swim and see what we can see.

Well, it is certain that the Senator did NOT cross on the ferry. And if he didn't swim....? Well, still another report that did not find its way into the inquest was that a motorboat perhaps a little more than fifteen feet in length with three persons aboard was sighted in the Edgartown harbor about a half-hour later than the alleged swim. It was approaching a moored sailboat when, just after having been spotted, its lights and motor were suddenly cut.[12] This proves nothing, of course, not even with an-

[11] Ibid. p. 83.
[12] Teddy Bare, p. 82-83.

other verifiable report that earlier that night a boat was stolen, but this is offered by some as the reason the Senator was seen at the Shiretown Inn at 2:25 a.m. in dry clothing (See Anomaly R).

What it is that imparts a lingering quality to these irrelevancies is portions of the testimonies of the Lyons sisters, Maryellen and Ann (or Nance). When asked about conversation with Messrs. Gargan and Markham after their return to the cottage at about 2:00 a.m., Maryellen said:[13]/

A: We, you know, when they arrived, we asked them, you know, where they had been; what had happened. Oh, it was just, "Oh, don't even ask us, we have been looking for boats." It was confused.
Q: That they had been looking for boats, they said that?
A: That was one of the things they said,...

And Nance replied thusly:[14]/

Q: Did Mr. Markham or Mr. Gargan indicate why Mr. Kennedy decided to swim when boats were available? (Could he have meant the ferry? --Auth.)
A: They said that they had been looking for a boat and couldn't find one.
Q: They, meaning Mr. Kennedy, Mr. Gargan and Mr. Markham?
A: Mr. Gargan and Mr. Markham, I believe.
Q: Had been looking for a boat?
A: Yes.
Q: But not Mr. Kennedy?
A: I don't--you know, they just said, you know, "We were looking for a boat."
Q: Was the purpose of the boat to assist the people at the party to get across, did you know?
A: No, I would assume that this was among the three involved.

Unfortunately the above (especially the last response) calls for more digging. We must ask why, and seek for the answer, such a boat if found would not have been for the benefit of all? As it was, ten persons (five men and five women) slept very uncomfortably in two rather small rooms. But merely by reviewing, one answer may be found for those willing to accept it in the Senator's well known humanitarian proclivities. He was simply, but bravely, striving to prevent further possible loss of life and/or serious injury. You see, had a boat been found (other than the ferry--at 1:30-2:00 a.m.?) and the Valiant returned for the remainder of the party, making several trips if necessary, the question of Mary Jo's whereabouts would certainly have arisen, as well as why just the Valiant? The truth could not have been long suppressed and.... well, the Senator told us his fears in his response footnoted 25, page 18.[15]/

---
[13]/ The Inquest. p. 102; see also p. 103.
[14]/ Ibid. p. 109.
[15]/ The Senator evidently cared naught for the safety of Messrs. Crimmins, Tretter and LaRosa. But perhaps none of these gentlemen were long and dear friends of Mary Jo's.

ANOMALY R (p. 15)

The "tourist" was Russell E. Peachey, innkeeper of the Shiretown, whose testimony included the following.

A: (Describing a portion of the Inn) ...The second floor has three units plus the deck ... Mr. Kennedy was on the second floor occupying space that entered off the deck area.
Q: Did you have occasion to see him sometime on the 19th?
A: I just happened to be standing in front of the office... and I heard footsteps coming across the deck. There were no lights up there, so I just thought I would wait to see who it might be, whether the person had any business being up there or not; and the individual came down the steps, and as he (the Senator) touched the ground, he turned around the steps and I asked if I could help him.
Q: Did you recognize him?
A: It wasn't until I spoke to him that I realized who it was.
Q: There are no lights on the deck?
A: There is a light up there, but it seemed to me that someone had switched it off. I can't really say whether that light was on or not. If it is, it is kind of a floodlight that is focused down to the floor of the deck right near where the steps enter up on the deck and it is purely to light the steps just slightly up there.
Q: So what did this person say?
A: I asked if I could help him. He said, "No." ... He said he had been awakened by a noise coming from a party next door. He went to look for his watch, he couldn't find it, and wondered what time it was. I turned and looked in the office.
Q: He was _awakened_?
A: Right.
Q: What did you do?
A: I turned and looked in the office window at the clock and I told him it was 2:25.
Q: What did this person do?
A: Thanked me, turned and went back to the quarters.

The reader is now requested to read ahead as far as footnote 20 in the testimony, page 16. What can be more obvious than that one of these two gentlemen demonstrated a disregard for the truth? At least, the compleat truth? Reverting to the preceding response of the Senator's, there was no mention of anything but retaining full consciousness prior to the confrontation with Mr. Peachey. If he had not been awakened, as he claimed, what was his motive for making the false statement? (According to Mr. Peachey's account, is a furtiveness apparent here?) And if Mr. Peachey falsified, what could he possibly have expected to gain, or what could he have attempted to conceal? It may help the reader to decide which of the two accounts to accept by reviewing some of the respective testimonies.

By the way, with a throbbing headache does it seem more logical to look for an aspirin than trying to find out what time it is?

ANOMALY S (p. 16)

Let us avail ourselves again of the testimony of Ralph Hewitt, the ferry operator who was on duty Saturday morning, July 19, 1969. Mr. Hewitt had stated that he had taken Senator Kennedy and two other gentlemen (one of whom he recognized as Mr. Markham) to Chappaquiddick. Mr. Fernandes asked further--[16]

Q: And could you tell us where they went on Chappaquiddick?
A: They didn't go very far. They stood around the point over there.
Q: Well, how long were you in their company or in their vicinity?
A: Oh, I would say approximately 20 minutes or so.
Q: And how did you measure this time to be 20 minutes?
A: Well, I figured that I made two or three trips in between the time I took them over and the time I took them back.
Q: Do you know what they were doing?
A: They appeared to be just milling around, waiting for something or someone.
THE COURT: Did you see anyone use the telephone?
THE WITNESS: No, I didn't.
Q: They were not in the telephone area?
A: They were in the telephone area...within 50 feet of the telephone.
Q: Did you have a conversation with Mr. Bettencourt?
A: Yes.
Q: What did he tell you?
A: He told me that the car that went off the Dike Bridge had been identified as Mr. Kennedy's.
Q: And then did anyone relay that to Mr. Kennedy?
A: Yes--or not to Mr. Kennedy, but to Mr. Markham.
Q: And who did that?
A: I did.
Q: What did you tell Mr. Markham?
A: I asked him if he was aware of the accident and he said, "Yes, we just heard about it."
Q: And after you relayed that information to them, what did you do?
A: I had passengers on the ferry; I went back and went to Edgartown.
Q: Did they go back with you?
A: Yes.
Q: How long after you relayed that information?
A: Within a couple of minutes.

One must suppose, I suppose, that it took the information that the car had been discovered and it was therefore generally known for Senator Kennedy to "fully realize" what had happened. THEN he immediately reported the matter to the police, as he said in his statement a little later at the Police Station (p. 17). In The Bridge at Chappaquiddick (p. 131), we are given a slightly different, but more

---
[16] The Inquest, p. 81.

compleat and deftly recounted version of this excursion.

The Mr. Bettencourt referred to is presented as a well known personality in the environs of Edgartown and the recognized authority on the tides at Poucha Pond. (It was he who predicted that it would be slack that day at approximately 11:30 a.m., and thus it was.) Mr. Bettencourt had heard the news, also, and had come over in his car on the ferry. He recognized the Senator and walked over to the threesome and informed Mr. Kennedy of the fact and even offered him a lift to the bridge. It was declined, however, the reason given to Mr. Bettencourt being that he (the Senator) was returning to Edgartown.

But return immediately, he did not. Mr. Hewitt did not hear this brief exchange of words, and after the mentioned two or three trips he decided Senator Kennedy must still be ignorant of the tragedy and approached them. Mr. Kennedy, one would surmise, was not anxious to engage in conversation with Mr. Hewitt, as he managed to keep a little distance between them and he seemed to be gaining. Not easily daunted, however, Mr. Hewitt called out and asked if he had heard about the accident, but the people's White Knight had taken refuge among some cars that were parked in the area. At this point, former United States Attorney Paul Markham, in a flash of a flanking movement, leaped into the breach with his line, "Yes, we just heard about it." Mr. Hewitt was forced to retreat to the ferryboat at this and made preparations for the return trip. The Senator was quickly persuaded to come out of seclusion and they all went back to Edgartown on the very next trip. Upon arrival, Mr. Kennedy literally leaped ashore and was so determined to get to the Police Station with an absolute minimum of dribbling of the sands of time that he nearly knocked someone over who innocently, if carelessly, found himself in his path. (See photo, p. 11B, Time, Aug. 1, 1969.)

ANOMALY T (p. 17)

Someone connected with the inquest must have had reason to be curious about telephone calls the Senator might have made because a summons was issued to the New England Telephone and Telegraph Company, which was responded to by their general accounting supervisor, A. Robert Malloy, who followed Senator Kennedy on the witness stand. Mr. Malloy was accompanied by Charles R. Parrott, Esq., attorney in behalf of the Telephone Company.

Even Judge Boyle had a little difficulty with some of Mr. Malloy's responses that concerned the Telephone Company's billing system. After shaking out the ashes, telephone subscribers can have any number of billing account numbers they wish (if they can afford it) all over the country. Moreover, any number of credit cards can be issued, authorized by the subscriber, of course, making telephone calls chargeable by holders of these cards to that specific number. Mr. Kennedy has such a credit card and he has several billing account numbers, as well. Mr. Malloy said he had been able to investigate "three of (Mr. Kennedy's) accounts, one in Boston, one in Washington and one in Virginia." He brought with him only the original records for Boston, however, and it was understood that this number was in

person(s) made the first two calls on that date. Who made them may be unimportant, or why, as well as who made the 6:30 p.m. call. ~~None of the other witnesses testioned making any phone calls however~~.

It also seems reasonable to infer that there had been a number of calls and that Mr. Malloy had a fair stack of those operator's original call cards; otherwise, why should there have been a compilation of a sheet of paper? And only four, selected at random (?), received notice and comment? Mr. Kennedy did quite a bit of telephoning later that Saturday morning, and so did Mr. Markham, according to Jack Olsen.[18] This was from the Police Station. In fact, requesting to use a telephone was the first thing the Senator did upon his arrival, and Mr. Olsen tells us further that the then future Senate "whip" was so nervous during a part of this time that he required assistance in dialing. Moreover, a number of these calls (both by Mr. Kennedy and Mr. Markham) were to points in several other states. It seems reasonable, also, that the twenty-four-minute call begun at 10:57 was made by the Senator to Mr. and Mrs. Kopechne. Some of the other frantic calls no doubt concerned getting Mary Jo's body off the island as quickly as possible, but let Zad Rust[19] tell you about that.

And did anyone overlook Mr. Parrott's phrase that Mr. Malloy had "just about all" of the cards with him? Can there be any other conclusion but that both Mr. Malloy and Mr. Parrott were concealing o t h e r calls of which both had knowledge? His Honor overlooked it. Consider the brief colloquy that immediately followed the last response:

THE COURT: Do you want to offer this as an exhibit?
MR. DINIS: Well, your Honor, I don't see any harm in offering it for the record.
THE COURT: It doesn't at the moment tell me anything.
MR. DINIS: No, it doesn't, and it may not, but we will make it part of the record.
THE COURT: Exhibit No. 4, I believe.

One reason the records didn't tell his Honor anything at that moment or at any later moment may have been that no further questions were asked, not of the Senator nor of any of the several witnesses who followed. Such questions might have been for example: Who besides the Senator held credit cards billable to his account, in Boston and/or elsewhere?. Who made any of the numerous calls, to whom, and why?

More important, his Honor displayed no interest whatever in calls that might have been charged to either his Washington account or the one in Virginia. We may deduce, then, that the "someone" who was curious about telephone calls emanating from Martha's Vineyard on those two days that were directly connected with Senator Edward Kennedy was not the Honorable James A. Boyle.

But there was other interest; active interest. And some of the other active interest was outside the judiciary machinery of

---
[18] The Bridge at Chappaquiddick, p. 138, 139.
[19] Teddy Bare, p. 35-39.

the Southern District of Massachusetts. One such interested person was Ralph Clifford, editor-publisher of the New York Graphic, a small newspaper published in New York City. Mr. Clifford made up in personal courage for the limited circulation of his struggling periodical when he came out with an "extra" edition on October 6, 1969, carrying the following headlines: 12 KENNEDY PHONE CALLS DETAILED BY N.Y. GRAPHIC. In the feature story, it was revealed that a total of 17 calls were made that were charged to Senator Kennedy's Washington, D.C. office, although only 12 were being detailed. Yes, they all emanated from the area of Edgartown, several of them from the Shiretown Inn -- (617) 627-4183 -- and a few from -- guess what? --the COOK-OUT COTTAGE!

Yes, dear reader, according to that feature story in the New York Graphic, there was a telephone in the cook-out cottage -- (617) 627-4020. (A typesetter's error listed it as 527-4020. Mr. Malloy explained in his testimony that the digits 617 indicated the Edgartown area.) Slightly abridged, the Graphic detailed the 12 calls as follows, the first three having been from the cottage:

First Call
The first call we were able to pinpoint was made at 11:57 p.m., Friday, July 18, to (212) 935-8790 in New York City, an unlisted number, which is registered in the name of Theodore Sorenson,[20] who was a special assistant to President John F. Kennedy. The duration of the call was two minutes.

Second Call
The frightened callers placed the second call at 12:04 a.m., Saturday, July 19, to Hyannisport, Mass., to (617) 775-4732. This is an unlisted number at 165 Greenwood, Hyannisport, a house once used by the Kennedy family and presently utilized by them as an office facility. The call lasted six minutes.

Third Call
Eight minutes later, another urgent call was placed to the same number in Hyannisport and the conversation consumed 18 minutes.

It is assumed that after this last call from the cottage that the midnight callers "borrowed" a boat ride, or "swam", as the Senator claims he did, to Edgartown. An odd coincidence, reported by the Manchester (N.H.) Union Leader's investigative reporter, Arthur E. Egan, Jr., is that a power boat was reported "stolen" that night. It was recovered less than 200 yards from the Shiretown Inn, where the Senator was registered.

Fourth Call
There were no further calls made until 2:54 a.m., when the apprehensive callers dialed (202) 233-9600. This is the Washington, D.C. office of Marshall & Hamilton, at 1825 K St., N.W. It is believed that this four-minute call was made to contact Burke Marshall, Senator Kennedy's Washington attorney. Marshall is a former Assistant U.S. Attorney General.

---

[20] Ibid., p. 43, previously cited.

Fifth Call

At 5:04 a.m., the Marshall & Hamilton office was called again and the conversation period was three minutes.

Sixth Call

At 5:54 a.m., which indicates the nervous callers were awake throughout the night, a call was placed to (202) 393-3111, the telephone number of Kennedy's brother-in-law, Stephen Smith, in Washington. This significant call consumed 27 minutes.

Seventh Call

At 5:28 a.m., the dismayed callers at the Shiretown Inn telephoned Theodore Sorenson again and spoke for 21 minutes, a possible indication that the Kennedy advisor had been surely reached.

Mr. Sorenson was quoted in the establishment's controlled press on August 25 as having denied that telephone calls were made in the early hours of July 19, after the incident. Mr. Sorenson stated, "No telephone calls were made that night, and since I was supposedly the recipient to two of them, I'm in the position to know."

Such existing knowledge of long-distance calls are placed to Mr. Sorenson obviously proves the inaccuracy of his statement. (The preceding sentence is verbatim from the story. Its awkward structure indicates another typesetter's error, or some such similarity.--Auth.)

Eighth Call

At 6:04 a.m., again in the early hours of July 19, the anxious callers again dialed (212) 935-8790, Mr. Sorenson's private number, and the length of this conversation was seven minutes.

Ninth Call

The next call, placed at 6:56 a.m., lasting one minute only, was the third call made to (202) 223-9600, the Washington, D.C. number for Burke Marshall. Evidently, Mr. Marshall was still unavailable, or perhaps uncooperative.

Tenth Call

At 7:19 a.m., a fourth call was placed to Burke Marshall. The length of the call was two minutes.

Eleventh Call

Nearly an hour later, at 8:14 a.m., Theodore Sorenson was called for what was evidently the fourth time. The conversation which took place this call lasted 42 minutes, the longest call of the night.

Twelfth Call

Brother-in-law Stephen Smith was again called for the second time at 9:01 a.m. This call consumed 11 minutes.

To be sure, a couple of anomalies appear in this detailing besides the digital error in the cottage telephone number. The careful observer may already have noticed that the sixth and sev-

calls alleged to have been made--four of them. (Who accepted those calls at a business office at those hours? Or is there one of those nighttime automatic switching devices that relays incoming calls to another number?) And then there was the acknowledged call to Mr. Smith and the two the Graphic claims were made.

Suppose we take this 9:01 call and develop it from the standpoint of all visible ramifications. The Senator admitted having made one call after eight o'clock to Mr. Smith to find out Burke Marshall's telephone number (after having made four earlier ones) from the public telephone at the Shiretown Inn. Did this require eleven minutes? Assuming complete error on the part of the Graphic for the sake of argument for the moment, did the Senator never hear of calling Directory Assistance (formerly "Information") to obtain telephone numbers in distant cities? It's easy. You dial: (area code) 555-1212. Instructions are usually in every public telephone booth or on the telephone instrument. This call matches with the Graphic. At 9:12, Messrs. Kennedy, Gargan and Markham sprinted to the ferry slip just down the street, and arrived there probably by 9:15, where the ferry was luckily waiting. This is close enough to ferry operator Ralph Hewitt's estimate of "in the vicinity of 9:00 o'clock" as the time the triumvirate came aboard. (Would anyone like to guess why both Messrs. Gargan and Markham were necessary as traveling companions to make a phone call?) The ferry run is no more than 200 yards across, and even if the current was swift on that crossing we could expect an arrival and debarking at Chappaquiddick of no later than 9:20-9:25. Now we add the "20 minutes or so" Mr. Hewitt says they were "just milling around" on the point over there and we get 9:45 as the latest for casting off, Edgartown-bound. This would allow time for the Senator to reach the Police Station, as he guessed, "some time before 10:00." It is also very near the ferry slip.

But we have to go back to Chappaquiddick and we have to review a little in past testimony now. At the opening of the Afternoon Session, Mr. Kennedy said he had made a phone call from Chappaquiddick with the "intention of reaching Mr. Burke Marshall", but that he had not reached him. Now let's go back to the discussion of Anomaly S (p. 43) and recall the Court asking Mr. Hewitt if he saw anyone use the telephone. "No, I didn't", was the reply, although they were "within 50 feet of the telephone." The defense against this is so simple that the Senator's chief counsel at the inquest, Edward B. Hanify, Esq., would doubtless delegate it to a junior associate: Senator Kennedy had not been under constant surveillance by Mr. Hewitt during this period and the call had been made, or attempted, during one of the several runs back to Edgartown that had been acknowledged and when Mr. Hewitt obviously could not have observed it. Ah, so. Nolo contendere. But did this take 20 minutes?

Now we must reach ahead for bits of the testimony of Messrs. Gargan and Markham regarding this signal event. With Mr. Gargan on the stand, Mr. Dinis asked: [23]

Q: Now, did you have any conversation with the Senator and Mr. Markham on the Chappaquiddick landing that morning?
A: No, not to any great degree. The Senator did all the talk-

---
[23] Ibid., p. 37.

the Senator's name, alone. Mr. Dinis asked:[17]

> Q: Now, with regard to your records, do they show any calls emanating from Chappaquiddick or Edgartown?
> A: Yes, they do, sir.
> Q: Will you produce the records that show those specific calls emanating from Edgartown or Chappaquiddick for those particular dates, July 18th and July 19th?
> MR. PARROTT: If I may address the Court at this point, your Honor, there is some primary evidence...or basic cards that are made by the telephone operator at the time the call is placed. Mr. Malloy has just about all of these with him as to calls originating in the New England area... To assist the Court, he has made a compilation which I think would be helpful..in their chronological time sequence from July 18th to July 19th.
> Q: Would you explain this sheet showing the calls that were made as to what times of the day they were made?
> A: Yes, sir. Like this first one-- On the 18th, was made at 10:08 a.m. and it lasted for one minute and 20 seconds. That was a call from Edgartown...to Arlington, Virginia.
> Q: That this (another call.--Auth.) was made at 12:30 p.m. that day?
> A: That is right.
> Q: This at 6:39 p.m.?
> A: That evening, yes, sir.
> On the 19th, the first one was 10:57 (a.m.).
> Q: And that call lasted 23 minutes?
> A: Twenty-three minutes and 54 seconds, sir.
> THE COURT: I ask this question now. You do not require the person initiating the call to identify himself?
> THE WITNESS: No, sir.
> THE COURT: In other words, anyone can use my credit card if they know the number?
> THE WITNESS: Yes, sir.

For so brief an interrogation (even without a small amount of judicious editing, in the author's opinion), the foregoing is fairly burgeoning with anomalies. First, let us note that although the records could pinpoint calls emanating from either Chappaquiddick or Edgartown, the initiating point, (Edgartown) of only the first call was mentioned, along with the distant point. And it is most noteworthy that not only do those operator's original call cards indicate the originating city or area, with the distant point, they show the precise number of the telephone instrument from which the call was made, along with the distant number called. What this means, simply, is that the pinpointing with respect to location can be very exact. It is recommended that this be remembered, as it will assume greater significance a little later on.

Next, since the Senator did not arrive in Edgartown until approximately one o'clock Friday afternoon, the 18th, we may safely infer that at least one other member of the party who arrived earlier was a credit card holder for his Boston number and that that

---
[17] Ibid. p. 13.

enth calls are in reverse order. Neither of these is hardly worth
mentioning, they are so minor, but Kennedy-campers are certain to
pounce on the overlapping of times between the properly placed seventh call (5:54 to 6:21) and the eighth call, which began at 6:04
and ended at 6:11. The obvious question generated by this information is how Mr. Kennedy, or anyone else, could have made that
eighth call when he was still carrying on the seventh and did not
hang up until ten minutes after the eighth call was supposed to
have terminated? That looks like a real stickler and no claim is
made here for the absolute answer, but two reasonable conjectures
can be offered. The first is that the eighth call was made by another party than the one engaged in the seventh. Who this might
have been is an open question. Is it possible that one of the
other five men went back to Edgartown with the Senator, theirs and
other testimony notwithstanding? (Perjury was commonplace during
that inquest.) It is doubtful. The one remaining, visible candidate is Joseph Kennedy III, the Senator's 'teen-aged nephew. Young
Joe certainly was in Edgartown that night, Jack Olsen[21] tells us,
which appears to be supported by the District Attorney's interest,
when questioning Mr. Kennedy, in whether Joe III had also stayed at
the Shiretown Inn. "Not to my knowledge", was the reply.[22]

The alternate possibility seems at the moment to be the more
plausible. That is, that the 5:54 call to Mr. Smith did not last
27 minutes, but only seven. And it would also seem that the error
in the length of the call occurred before it reached the Graphic.

Pursuing this avenue, let us note that the eighth call was to
Mr. Sorenson (who later defended the trip to Chappaquiddick to make
a telephone call) and it is doubtful that anyone but the Senator
would have conversed with that gentleman for seven minutes. Could
it have been advantageous to have both parties on the line simultaneously? Perhaps, but this would have required two separate and
virtually adjacent telephone instruments, unless a "conference"
call was arranged, which is most unlikely. An informational squib
abridged from the detailing of the sixth call, above, seems to fit
well enough with the deductive speculation that the error was in
the length of the call. It was: "Throughout the past decade, Mr.
Smith publicly has been referred to as an 'errand boy' for the Kennedy brothers." How does one justify conversing at six o'clock on
a Saturday morning (even this one) for 27 minutes with his errand
boy?' And it was hardly a family chat.

Whatever the explanation for these detailing anomalies, errors of greater magnitude and consequence have been committed in
publications of greater magnitude. And if the Presidential Hopeful
("Happiness is Kennedy in '72"--or at least in '76) was so nervous
at the Police Station as to require assistance in dialing, may we
not assume some understandable trepidation on the part of those involved in making this information public and been so affected by it?
Let it be remembered that the date of this issue of the Graphic was
almost exactly three months prior to the beginning of the inquest,
and let us note the things that do line up properly, such as the admitted desire and attempt to call Burke Marshall and the actual

---

[21] The Bridge at Chappaquiddick, section,'The Edgartown Regatta.'
[22] The Inquest, p. 3.

ing and that was basically on the phone. After he finished, I think it was I that suggested that Paul go with him to the Police Station; that I would go to the cottage, tell the girls what had happened and take them back to the Katama.

And Mr. Markham obliged with this version:24/

A: The Senator wanted to know where he could call. He said he didn't want to use that phone at the hotel there. He wanted some degree of privacy and there were going to be people around. So, Joe told him that there was a telephone on the Chappaquiddick side.
Q: And so you went with him to the ferry and crossed to Chappaquiddick?
A: Right.
Q: And what happened there?
A: He called Dave Burke.
Q: He called Dave Burke?
A: Right.
Q: Did he speak with him, do you know?
A: Yes.
Q: And do you know whether or not he called Mr. Marshall?
A: No, I don't think he called Mr. Marshall. He only called Mr. Burke and asked Mr. Burke to try to get ahold of Mr. Marshall and he wanted to talk to him and just to stand by. The place was going to be flooded with calls pretty soon and to get down to the office and to notify Burke Marshall.
Q: Then what did he do?
A: Then he concluded the telephone conversation. I said, "Do you want me to go to the Police Station with you?" He said, "Yes." He said, "Joe, you had better go tell the others what happened."

Isn't it interesting that none of these three mentioned the brief confrontations with Messrs. Bettencourt and Hewitt? The first, in particular, having been omitted, why was it anticipated that "the place was going to be flooded with calls pretty soon"? And if the name, Dave Burke, is new to the reader, Mr. Burke is an administrative assistant to Mr. Kennedy, and it may be noteworthy that at no point in his testimony did the Senator mention Mr. Burke.

Should we ask why it took some twenty minutes to make a phone call, the time Mr. Hewitt estimated they were there? It did not take that long. Let's remember that they appeared to be "just milling around, waiting for something or someone." Could that "something" have been an <u>incoming</u> phone call? --perhaps from the much sought Mr. Marshall, resulting from the 9:01 call to brother-in-law Stephen Smith? That would certainly establish the previous knowledge not only of the existence ~~of the existence~~ of the telephone on the Chappaquiddick side, but the number that might have been given to Mr. Smith for relay to Mr. Marshall (remember the "swim" and the "looking for boats" matter?).

24/ Ibid., p. 47,48.

So, may we surmise that perhaps the original intention in going to Chappaquiddick was to <u>receive</u> and not to make a phone call and that, if one was indeed made, it was after Mr. Bettencourt enlightened the Senator regarding the discovery at Dike Bridge? In this vein, remember that the ferry made two or three round trips before Mr. Hewitt catalyzed them into returning.

Now we flashback to Mr. Malloy, as he explained the information on the sheet concerning "just about all" of the calls that emanated from the Edgartown area that were billed to the Senator's Boston account: "On the 19th, the <u>first</u> one was 10:57." That was approximately approximately an hour and a half after the time of the alleged call from Chappaquiddick and almost two hours after the one from the Shiretown Inn (9:01) "to get Mr. Marshall's number." And we recall that, although he had examined the records of Mr. Kennedy's Washington and Virginia billing accounts as well, he had brought only those records of calls charged to his Boston number. Or would you prefer to believe that both the call from the Shiretown and the one from Chappaquiddick a half hour later (?) were paid for in nickels, dimes and quarters? (Let this be perfectly clear before leaving this discussion: Both Messrs. Malloy and Parrott are honorable men--so are they all, all honorable men (and women).)

Now another flashback--to the discussion of Anomaly R (p. 42). Do you still believe the Senator didn't know what time it was, that he couldn't find his watch, dressed and went out looking for a clock or someone with a watch? Or would you rather believe he was looking for a telephone? (The Shiretown evidently does not have telephones in each room, or the switchboard was understandably closed at that hour; else, why should the 9:01 call have been from a public phone?) Would the Senator want to admit this to Mr. Peachey, whom he neither expected nor wanted to meet? After Mr. Kennedy returned to his room (with the knowledge of the time), did he wait a half-hour for Mr. Peachey to leave for the night, then go back down to the deserted lobby and make the 2:54 a.m. call in an attempt to reach his dear old friend, Burke Marshall? Did he then return to his room for a couple of hours, where he "almost tossed and turned" and paced the room wondering what to do about the accident and grieving for the loss of a devoted friend?

Whatever the answers to these questions, do you have a better understanding of why the Senator said (footnoted 19, p. 15) that he "never really went to bed that night?"

By the way, if his watch wasn't waterproof, it wouldn't have done much good if he had found it. Or did he "forget" it early in the evening as he left for the cook-out? Or would it have been run down by that time, in any event?

ANOMALY U (p. 18)

This is one of several anomalies that must be shared with Senator Kennedy, Judge Boyle being one, the extent or degree being arbitrary. It refers, of course, to Mr. Dinis's having just asked Mr. Kennedy if he had, indeed, done what he claimed in his statement with regard to notifying the police. He was at the very swordpoint of having to face obvious perjury when his honor intervened, as he did on several other occasions.

What is more apparent than that the Senator had "fully realized" what had happened, even, for the sake of argument, accepting his questionable account of events? One of the defenses was an affidavit from Robert D. Watt, M.D., with offices at Cape Cod Medical Center, Hyannis. Dr. Watt stated that he had visited and examined Mr. Kennedy on July 19, 1969 (obviously, the afternoon) and diagnosed "concussion, contusions and abrasions of the scalp, acute cervical strain." He said further, "The diagnosis of concussion was predicated upon the foregoing objective evidence of injury and the history of the temporary loss of consciousness and retrograde amnesia. Impairment of judgment, and confused behavior are symptoms consistent with an injury of the character sustained by the patient." 25/ It is most apparent that Dr. Watt did not question the history as it was given.

Another conceivable defense is to draw a rough parallel with certain boxers, for example, who have been known to fight several rounds they were subsequently unable to recall. In such instances— and no doubt there are others not limited to boxing—the seemingly intelligent actions of the individuals were due largely to conditioned reflex. They were engaged in activities for which they had undergone intensive training as to courses of action under varying circumstances. In other cases, actions for which there was subsequent amnesia may have been due to extensive repetition, which is merely another form of conditioned reflex. But such was not the case here in either instance. Consider, for example, that rationality was required to go to the cottage for assistance, having recognized his own limitations. And let us recall a portion of his dramatic response, footnoted 17 on page 13, where he said, "A lot of different thoughts came into my mind at that time about now I was going to really to be able to call Mrs. Kopechne at some time in the middle of the night to tell her that her daughter was dead.." Is this not full realization? Does it indicate "confused behavior" when (he said) he instructed Messrs. Gargan and Markham "to take care of the girls" and that he would "take care of the accident" just before plunging into the channel at the ferry slip (?)? Had he been in a state of shock, with impaired judgment, would these two gentlemen not have noticed it immediately, such as when he gave "suggestions" to them in their diving attempts a full hour previously at the outset of the resumed attempted rescue operation? (See response footnoted 15, page 13.) And they had no qualms whatever about his ability to swim the channel.

In Edgartown, Mr. Peachey saw nothing unusual in his bearing or manner; it was what he was doing, not how (?), that had aroused his curiosity. Neither was there any suspicion of drunkenness.

As if the preceding were not enough, there was his behavior following daylight--those he met and talked with before the trip to Chappaquiddick (p. 15, following the response footnoted 19). Once again, Jack Olsen recounts in his finest style 26/ the casual, leisurely manner in which the Senator went about these early morning chance happenings. That, of course, was necessarily only hear-

---
25/ The Inquest, pp. 90,91.
26/ The Bridge at Chappaquiddick, section, "The Morning After."

say, but we can find sufficient evidence for credibility from two sources in testimony given at the inquest. The first of these was from Mr. Ross Richards, one of the Senator's yachting comrades, who also, by chance, had a room practically adjacent to Mr. Kennedy's at the Shiretown. Mr. Fernandes asked Mr. Richards: 27/

Q: Now, did you have occasion to see the Senator or Mr. Kennedy at approximately 7:30 on the 19th?
A: Yes, sir.
Q: Would you tell us where you saw him?
A: I was entering from Water Street, taking a left into the cottage at Shiretown and he was walking in a westerly direction towards me and I was walking in an easterly direction.
Q: And did you have a conversation with him at that time?
A: At that time we said, "Good morning", and he turned and I kept walking, nodded and said, "Good morning", and he turned and walked with me.
Q: What was the conversation at this time?
A: It was about the prior race the day before, I happened to win the race and he congratulated me on it and we discussed that back and forth for maybe ten or fifteen minutes.
Q: So you walked and discussed this matter and then you went up to the porch or deck which is adjoining both rooms and you also discussed this?
A: Right.
Q: How long were you in his company all told?
A: It was until 8:00 o'clock.
Q: So, would it be safe to say approximately half an hour?
A: Half an hour.
Q: And within this time you had conversation with him?
A: Yes.
Q: About the races and anything else?
A: And the weather. It was a nice day.
Q: Was there any discussion about Chappaquiddick Island?
A: There wasn't a word mentioned of Chappaquiddick.
Q: Were you joined by anyone?
A: Stanley Moore followed behind us and he was sitting on the porch with us.
Q: And he, too, shared in this conversation?
A: Yes, sir.
Q: Now, what observations, if any, did you make of the Senator at this time as to any injuries, his appearance or attitude?
A: I didn't notice anything out of the ordinary.
Q: You noticed nothing out of the ordinary in his speech?
A: In his speech, no.
Q: In appearance?
A: In appearance, no.
Q: Now, did anyone else join or come onto the deck during that time?
A: My wife came out around 7:50. She heard us talking out there and we were about to go to breakfast, so she came out and sat for five or ten minutes.

27/ The Inquest, pp. 38,39.

Q: Did anyone else come?
A: No, sir.
Q: Were you ever joined or see Mr. Markham or Mr. Gargan that morning?
A: Mr. Markham, Mr. Gargan-- I remember the bell at 8:00 o'clock. It rang and we asked the Senator if he would like to have breakfast with us and he said, no, he wouldn't, but he may join us later, and at that time Mr. Markham and Mr. Gargan--
Q: May I stop you? -- You said the Senator discussed the possibility of joining you at breakfast later?
A: Later.
Q: And then you say Mr. Markham and Mr. Gargan came on the deck?
A: Yes, sir.
Q: What happened when they came up on the deck?
A: They went directly to the Senator's room and opened the door and he followed them into the room.
Q: Did you see them confer?
A: No, I didn't.
Q: They did not confer prior to entering the room?
A: They did not.
Q: Did you see them leave?
A: No, I didn't.

Later that day, Tuesday, Mr. Markham gave the following as his version of the episode.[28] It could not be as complete, but 'tis enough. He was asked where in the Shiretown he went upon returning to Edgartown that Saturday morning.

A: I went in along the side up into the back courtyard there. I went up the back stairs to the porch which was outside of the room, where the Senator's room--
Q: And where was the Senator when you saw him?
A: He was seated out on the porch at a table.
Q: Who was with you at this time?
A: Mr. Gargan.
Q: What did you do upon arriving there, what did you say?
A: I didn't say anything. I went up the steps. I saw the Senator seated there and it was obvious to me at that time that nothing had been done.
Q: Well, how was it obvious to you that nothing--
A: Well, there was no commotion. There was no--he was just seated there at the table.
Q: Alone?
A: No. I remember Mr. Richards being in the immediate vicinity and also another gentleman.
Q: Was it Mr. Moore?
A: Moore. Stan Moore, right.
Q: And did you have a conversation at that time?
A: At that point, no. I went directly to the door of the room where he was. It was locked. I think he told Joe Gargan that he

---
[28] Ibid., p. 47.

had left the key inside and closed the door and Joe went down and got another key and returned.

If this portion of Mr. Markham's testimony is the truth, the whole truth and nothing but the truth, and if the Senator's locking himself out of his room (who doesn't do this occasionally?) indicates confused behavior and impaired judgment, then we must accept Dr. Watt's opinion without question.

With further reference to Dr. Watts and his affidavit, and to strive to match Senator Kennedy's assiduousness and desire for completeness, it would be in order to mention that Judge Boyle rejected the affidavit "because he considered it to be immaterial and not pertinent."29/ With the affidavit subjected to close scrutiny, however, this rejection increases Judge Boyle's share in this anomaly, the exposition of which again requires a little review.

We must revert to Senator Kennedy's testimony, page 8, and the response footnoted 7. This, of course, was reiteration of the same declaration made in his statement at the Police Station (page 17), as well as in his famous radio/TV "explanation", which was, essentially, "I have no idea how I got out of that car." Dr. Watts mentioned "retrograde amnesia", it will be recalled (page 53, footnoted 25). Perhaps, like the "double floods" and "double ebbs" they have in the tides at Edgartown, there is something like "double retrograde." This will be more clearly understood (or will it?) if we refer to the specific "history" Dr. Watts referred to, apparently as it was given to him.30/

The history of the present illness was as follows: (the Senator) stated that he had been in an auto accident last night on Martha's Vineyard. The car went off a bridge. There is a lapse in his memory between hitting the bridge and coming to under water and struggling to get out. There was a loss of orientation--at the last moment, he grabbed the side of an open window and pulled himself out. He was not clear on the events following but he remembered diving repeatedly to check for a passenger--without success. He went for help and returned. Again, effort to rescue passenger was without success. He was driven to the ferry slip and swam to the main body of land. He went to his hotel where he slept fitfully until 7:00 a.m.

Retrograde amnesia? Well, in his talk with Dr. Watt, Mr. Kennedy evidently had amnesia for having told Police Chief Arena in that unsigned statement he collaborated with Mr. Markham on that he had "no recollection of how (he) got out of the car", and that was only a matter of hours earlier. Then, on radio/TV he reiterated the denial of how his escape came about, evidently having ex-

grams and sketches of his movements--where he dove, and the position of the submerged Oldsmobile in relation to the bridge. He experienced no difficulty in finding the cottage on foot. Just what kind of orientation did he lose?

And shall we note, again for the sake of compleatness, that in Dr. Watt's account the window was open, whereas, on the witness stand (page 7) he said the window was closed. (That he reversed this on the very next page and said it was open is further indication of "oscillating" amnesia.)

Finally (?), we note the statement that after returning to his hotel he "slept fitfully until 7:00 a.m." This is more anomalous, of course, but we must remember that Mr. Kennedy was not under oath when he gave that account to Dr. Watt. However, one may notice that he snapped out of it rather quickly and without much difficulty when Mr. Richards' testimony is considered.

This fits well enough in the schedule of telephone calls detailed by the New York Graphic, please note (Anomaly T). He met Mr. Richards at approximately 7:30 a.m., which means he could have just made the tenth call at 7:19. Then, after going into the room at approximately 8 o'clock, he could very easily have made the eleventh call, after conferring with Messrs. Gargan and Markham, at 8:14. This over at 8:56, he went downstairs and made the call from the public phone at 9:01. These first two calls mentioned, at 7:19 and 8:14, would be predicated on a telephone in the room and the switchboard now open. Mr. Tretter's testimony[31/] fits well enough, too, as he recounts how he unintentionally intruded into the room to find that it was a "private thing" and was requested to leave. This was a few minutes after eight.

There is an insistent question concerning this matter of the Senator notifying the police when he had "fully realized what had happened." First, however, a supposition or two are necessary. We recall that Mrs. Malm called the police because two boys had knocked on her door that morning and told her there was a car upside-down near the bridge. Then word got around rather quickly and Mr. Bettencourt heard about it, who, in turn, informed Senator Kennedy, who thereupon shortly after fully realized that his identity as owner of the car would become known from the license number being checked (it was, in fact). Now then, suppose the two boys had not decided to go fishing (that is what took them to the area) that Saturday morning and that no one had crossed the bridge. Or, suppose that, instead of being remarkably clear, the water around Martha's Vineyard was very muddy and the car had not been visible, not even at low tide.

Question: How long would it have been before the Senator decided to notify the police? If this question seems unusual, let us remember that he told Mr. Richards that he might join him and his wife for breakfast "later." And shall we also remember that the information first given out to the members of the party was simply that they "couldn't find Mary Jo?" She was "missing."

* * *

31/ Ibid., p. 18.

Rest in Peace

Mary Jo

Made in the USA
Las Vegas, NV
16 June 2023